FINDING

THE

WORDS

FINDING

THE

WORDS

Inge Israel

The publisher gratefully acknowledges the financial assistance of the Canada Council for the Arts and the Ontario Arts Council.

Library and Archives Canada Cataloguing in Publication

Israel, Inge, author
    Finding the words / Inge Israel.

ISBN 978-1-927079-40-9 (paperback)

    1. Israel, Inge. 2. Authors, Canadian--20th century--
Biography. I. Title.

PS8567.S73Z46 2016   C811'.54   C2016-904166-2

Editor: Bernadette Rule
Design and Typography: Rolf Busch
Inside Photograph: Shadows by Ralph Archibald

Published in 2016 by
Seraphim Editions
4456 Park Street
Niagara Falls, ON
L2E 2P6

Printed and bound in Canada

Acknowledgements

My heartfelt thanks to Werner and Pia without whose warm support, forbearance and love this book could never have been written; to Ralph who gently spurred me on; to Vivienne who never doubted me; to Allie, Sive, Peter and Garret for being with me in spirit.

My gratitude also to Maureen Whyte and Bernadette Rule, whose immediate understanding and kind encouragement helped me to "fill the gaps".

Some of these chapters, or earlier versions of them, have appeared in various publications. Thanks to the editors of:

Eating Apples, NeWest Press (Edmonton, Alberta): "The Beginning" published as "Uncertain Signs"

Le tableau rouge, Les Editions du Vermillon, (Ottawa, Ontario): "To Jean" published as "La main"

Le tableau rouge: "The King's Visit" published as "La visite du roi"

Antigonish Review #183: "The Window"

Imagine (Ireland), and *Garm Lu* (Toronto): "Auntie Moll"

BBC and CBC broadcast "Letter to Francis" as "The Red Painting"; it also appeared as the title story in *Le tableau rouge.*

Galleon Literary Journal (Cape Breton, Nova Scotia): "Sisters"

The Writers' Guild of Alberta Newsletter: "September, 1993, Letter to M."

Canadian Stories: A Literary Folk Magazine Written By or About Canadians (Fergus, Ontario): "Accident" published as "They Mess You Up ..."

Dedication

I would like to dedicate this book to my parents, my son Mark and my sister Paula, all of whom I miss so very much.

"May my dead be patient with the way my memories fade."
– Wyslawa Szymborska

"No, no, you're not thinking, you're just being logical."
– Niels Bohr.

CONTENTS

THE BEGINNING

Had my mother not finally said yes, my father would, on that epic journey out of Siberia, have been put into one of the front carriages of the train or one of those at the rear along with all the single ex-prisoners-of-war. The front carriages were blown apart by a mine and those at the rear were derailed by the impact. But she had said yes, so she and my father traveled in the relative safety of a middle carriage assigned to ex-prisoners who had married in Siberia. My father never forgot that she had, in this way, saved his life.

During her entire life my Russian mother spoke about her country, weaving a tapestry of its people and their culture with palpable nostalgia. No matter where, in the fabric of her vivid memories, I pull a thread, the tiny hole leads into another world, and I peer into it as I have always done, in an effort to understand. She never returned to her native Russia after she married my father and went to Germany with him. Fanny and Leo, my mother and father, met during the First World War while he was a prisoner-of-war in Siberia. And this was how it all began.

When the fighting spread into Russia, my mother's family fled to Siberia. She was the youngest and had not finished school when they left Vitebsk, the city of her birth. But in the Siberian village where her family settled and opened a small grocery store, being able to read and write placed her above most. In time, she became the teacher in the one-room village school and though she was not a trained nurse, she occasionally helped to tend the wounded brought there from the front. Her brothers sometimes visited the nearby internment camp where the prisoners-of-war were kept and brought them books or played chess with them. In this way they became acquainted with my father who, when not required to do prison chores, taught himself Russian and Esperanto. He also taught other willing prisoners Esperanto, convinced that if everyone spoke the same language there would be no more wars. He had hardly had time to see action at the front before being captured, but had seen enough.

My father's wish had been to become a mathematician but his parents could not afford to send him to university. Instead, since he was good with figures, they apprenticed him to a bank. Bored and frustrated, he ran away at the end of six months but there was nowhere to run and as a last resort he joined the army. He was not quite eighteen years old, but was recruited without being asked for proof of age. There was no time for instruction about firearms. He was shipped to the front at once and, within a few days, was taken prisoner and sent to Siberia.

Though conditions in the camp were harsh, prisoners were not ill-treated. They were even given postcards to "write home". But Siberia was soon completely cut off from the outside world, trains stopped running and mail service ceased. The prisoners' postcards could not be sent anywhere and my father used the blank side of his for sketches he made with an ink pencil. Some show accurate scenes of life at the camp, of a ring of prisoners pushing a big water-wheel, of men sitting on the ground delousing themselves, or using the latrines, etc. My mother kept these in an album and shortly before her death, gave them to me. Sadly, exposure to daylight rapidly caused them to fade. Unable to bear this second death, I retouched them myself. Now my father's lines and mine are intertwined.

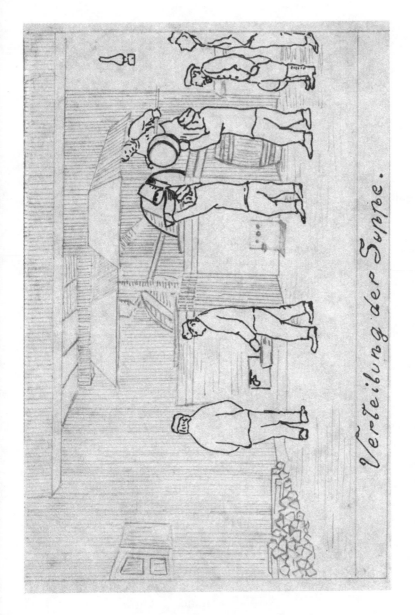

"Sharing out the soup"
Antipicha, 1915

"Our Home"
Antipicha, 1915

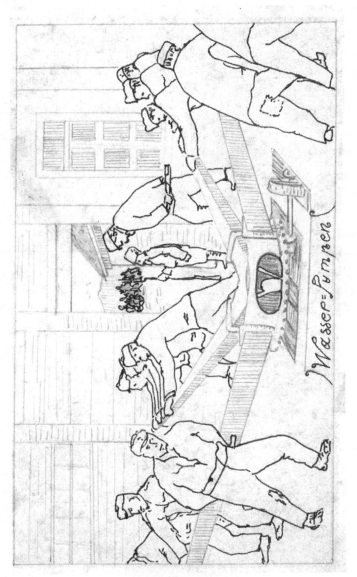

"Pumping Water"
Antipicha, 1915

When the war ended two years later my father could not go back to Germany. None of the ex-prisoners could be repatriated. Badly damaged trains and railway tracks, and especially the many unexploded mines still lodging along them, ruled out all travel. The internment camp was closed and the men were told to find work and lodgings. Villagers were encouraged to give them jobs and a place to sleep. My father became bookkeeper to a miller who had never kept books. The miller continued to mill his grain and count his sacks exactly as he had always done, taking no interest whatever in the figures my father conscientiously entered in a ledger. The payment for this work consisted of whatever the miller happened to have – a sack of grain or some other commodity that could then be used as barter. Once, the payment was a small live calf that my father proudly carried to my mother's family, having been invited by her brothers. He had not yet been introduced to my mother, but he had caught sight of her and she of him. From her window she now saw him approach, saw him struggle up the hill, hanging on as best he could to the jerking calf draped round his neck. She thought this hilarious and could not stop laughing even after he had arrived at the house – how devastated he must have felt!

Another two years passed before the railway tracks were restored. By the time my parents' dream of leaving Siberia together came true, my father had spent four years there. He was now twenty-two and my mother twenty. They married and boarded the very first overloaded train to carry prisoners-of-war out of the country. It crawled along uncertain tracks where mines, possibly unexploded, still lingered, stopping frequently for everyone to scramble off, not only to clear the tracks or get wood for the stoves that heated the carriages: there were no proper facilities on board, no water and soon, nothing to eat. The stops provided an opportunity to approach nearby farmers for necessities. Money had no value, but my mother had something to offer instead of worthless currency. Her parents had, with great foresight, given her some bags of salt – a precious commodity. This she was able to use as barter along the way. When everyone returned to their carriages, they shared whatever each had managed to get. It took them three months to cross the 3,500 kilometers from Siberia to Western Germany. For my parents it was one of a seemingly endless series of journeys to new existences. This first journey itself felt endless.

Already on the train my mother had begun to miss her family, to wish she could speak to them, tell them how it was with her, ask their advice. How could she have walked out on them? *They* would never have abandoned *her*. What would happen on this train? Would she be able to hold her own, day after day, night after night? And what monstrous thing awaited her at the end of this crazy journey?

As she recalled parting from them, questions that would henceforth haunt her sprang to mind. What had got into her? How could she have left her family and all those dear to her? Her mother had fainted. Her sisters had hurried her away. "Leave quickly! Don't linger! You'll only cause her more pain," they had said. When the train began to pull out of the station, they called after her, "Fanoutchka, take care!" But she had only felt a thrill of excitement. Dressed in fine new clothes, she was leaving for foreign parts with a clever, curly-headed man who loved her madly. Hadn't he threatened to take his own life if she did not agree to marry him? She had laughed, would not believe him at first – until he showed her the blade.

Whenever she thought back to that train journey from Siberia, my mother's cheeks felt hot: imagine traveling with a virtual stranger! And he was her husband! Squeezed into a carriage with so many other couples, she would not lie next to him. She hardly knew him, after all! And in front of all those people! Not that the others seemed to care. No shame! No modesty. But she would not. At night, she crawled on top of the stove, Russian fashion, to sleep. Up there she felt safe. The man who was now her husband was more of a stranger to her here than he had been among her own people. She could not understand what the other men were saying to him. They laughed a lot. At him? For not asserting his rights?

He looked embarrassed. Hardly spoke. Except to her. And mostly with his eyes. She felt sorry for him. But no. Not *that* sorry. Not here. Perhaps never. It looked ... sounded ... unspeakable.

But these concerns dwindled in importance when the train hit the mine. The front carriages blew up and most of those in them were killed. The rear carriages overturned from the impact and their occupants too were killed or seriously injured. All those who could, helped the injured, improvised first aid, tore clothes into bandages, stemmed the flow of blood. Whenever my mother spoke about this or other traumatic episodes in their lives, she relived the moment. The scenes she described of this event brought to mind Chagall's paintings showing upside down trains and people in mid-air, reinforcing the artist's connection with my mother. Chagall too was born in Vitebsk. They even attended the same school, though not at the same time.

She had been brought up mostly by her sisters since her parents were hardly ever at home. Her mother, my grandmother, left early in the morning to run their small grocery shop and only returned at night. Well, someone had to look after the customers! Earn the family's keep! Do what was necessary! My grandfather had no time for the shop. He spent his days in the prayer-house, studying the Talmud. When he arrived home, his daughters were expected to fetch and carry for him. He did not demand it; my grandmother did, on his behalf. At the prayer-house or on the way home, he often found some poor hungry man or a stranger with nowhere to go and brought him home to share whatever meal his daughters had prepared.

Without his knowledge, my grandmother often asked a non-Jewish neighbour to come into the house on Shabbat, to make some tea for herself, then offer my grandfather a cup. If it had been made specifically for him by a Jewish person on the holy Shabbat, he would have refused it. He was distant with his children and my mother hardly knew him but was afraid of him. She called it respect. Once a little fart escaped her just as he walked into the room. She was devastated, burst into hysterical laughter, could not stop until one of her sisters slapped her face. She never forgot that moment of shame.

I know my grandparents only from enlarged photographic portraits encased in heavy black frames. These were so important to my parents that they traveled everywhere with us, across borders and seas to hang on our walls, or stand propped against them. Sometimes I slept in the same room they occupied. My maternal grandmother had my mother's eyes. The same twinkle softened her face. I felt at ease with her. At her side my grandfather seemed quite harmless in spite of his beard, his black skullcap and the severe expression on his face.

But my paternal grandparents looked sinister to me. I could not come to terms with them, could not escape their piercing stare, felt it even through the cover I pulled over my head. Sometimes I got out of bed to turn this heavy picture toward the wall. It gave me recurrent nightmares: they were being placed in their coffins, they pushed against the lids while nails were being hammered in, calling out in choked voices, "We're not dead!"

Perhaps my mother had passed on to me some of the anxiety and apprehension she must have felt on arriving in Germany to meet her in-laws, clinging to her few precious possessions, fingering them nervously as I've so often seen her do. She would have been an outsider to them, someone who had stolen their eldest son. My father had tried to reassure her: they were simple folk, like her own. They had arrived in Germany from Poland without a cent, sold men's ties and suspenders from door to door. Gradually, from that hand-to-mouth existence, they had built up a small business. He was sure they would be happy to see her, to welcome her, he said. But in reality, how could he be sure of anything? He too was nervous about that first meeting. Had he not run away to join the army four years earlier without telling anyone, without saying goodbye? Would they forgive him? Accept him with his foreign bride?

When they arrived at the family home they learned that both his parents had died while he was in Siberia. Though my mother was spared the ordeal of meeting them, she often studied their stern faces in the photograph. Their spirit still reigned in the house. As wife of the eldest son, she was expected to carry on from where her husband's parents had left off. She was younger than her new brothers-in-law, the same age as one sister-in-law and only one year older than the youngest. Yet, as the eldest son's wife, it was she who had to take over the mother's role and responsibilities now.

The welcome that my father's brothers and sisters extended to my mother was doubtful. They looked on her as a curiosity and insisted on burning all her clothes, claiming that anything from such a primitive country as Russia was bound to be unclean. They threw her entire trousseau into the flames! Garments lovingly sewn and assembled by her mother and sisters! How could they have done such a thing? Oh, the horror of it! She was at least as clean as they were! She could not understand them and they could not understand her. And her husband was helpless, could do nothing to stop them.

Now in Frankfurt, my mother desperately missed her gentle mother, her bossy sisters, her stern father. She even missed the children whom she had taught in the village school. She felt older, more mature than her new sisters-in-law whom she compared unfavourably to those unspoiled, uncomplicated Siberian children. They had looked up to her, though she was small and dark-featured. My mother was short, had black hair and brown eyes, while everyone else in her family was tall, fair and grey-eyed. She was the youngest of six children and they had teased her, told her she did not really belong with them. In her secret moments, she wondered whether it was true. Perhaps this nagging doubt had made the decision to leave them easier. Of course, she had not then known that it would be forever.

Homesickness finally overwhelmed her when she became pregnant with her first child, my sister. She was still very much the foreigner in Germany. With new life forming in her womb, the longing to be among her own flesh and blood became vital and she tried to run away. She made it as far as the border, but was stopped there. Her papers were no longer valid, they said, and she was turned back. Oh, the despair of that surrender! Who could have imagined that one's entire life would depend on a slip of paper? At this point she was overcome with emotion and the whole tapestry of her recollections shook with her. The humiliation at having to return to my father's house! To face, not only him, but his brothers and sisters who would also demand an explanation. And yet she owed them nothing, would never forgive them for what they had done! Never, as long as she lived!

My father did not reproach her for her attempted escape. Just having his Fanoutchka back was all that mattered, finding her waiting for him again when he got home from work, seeing her again as she had been when he first met her. Even here in Frankfurt she had, on happy days, run joyfully about the house and jumped, yes, jumped across coffee tables ... though perhaps she could not do this now while pregnant. Pregnant with his child! The happiness of it! Surely she would soon laugh and sing again ... Why did she feel caged? She had all the freedom in the world and more comfort than she could have imagined in her wildest dreams. In Siberia she did not even know what a tap was, had never seen running water.

After my older sister was born, my mother finally accepted her life in a country whose culture and values so vastly differed from her own. The business that my father and his brothers had inherited from their parents had prospered and my mother now had a maid, Gikka. They were good friends, she and Gikka – a country girl whose train journey to the city was the first in her life; so excited by it, she wished that she and the train were alone in the world, traveling on forever; a girl who had never seen bananas before, and wrote home to her family about the "sweet yellow sausages" from Africa. My mother understood her, could sympathize and identify with her. In the kitchen with Gikka, where there was no pretence, she felt completely at ease. When guests came to the house, she found "urgent" things to do in the kitchen.

To the end of her life, she was only comfortable in the company of simple folk, those who related to the earth, or to one another on a compassionate human level, those whom she judged to be "genuine" people. She went out of her way to avoid the pompous, the self-serving, the greedy.

An impressionable teenager back in Russia, young Fanny had stood on boxes or perched on walls, all ears, to listen to the impassioned speeches of revolutionaries. With deep emotion they spoke of the unfairness of the prevailing feudal system. They promised radical change. There would be no more poor, no more underdogs, they cried! They would bring equality to all men and women, ensure that all riches were distributed equally. Wealth was evil! Possessions were evil if they deprived others! Money was dirty! These slogans became deeply ingrained in my mother's mindset. They remained with her until the end.

Now, now! my father would say to her, shaking his head in a familiar gesture. Thoughtful, quiet, infinitely patient and deeply in love with this small, dark-eyed, dynamic woman, he never tired of pointing out to her the truth as he saw it. Endlessly, he repeated how much better everything was in a modern country among reliable, honest people. In Russia he had been robbed several times of the little he possessed, even from under his pillow while he slept! In Russia nothing functioned because there was no work ethic, no discipline. In Russia the New Order claimed to equalize society, but instead took away all freedom. The New Order was a utopian dream that could never be put into practice because mankind simply was not ready.

"That's not true!" my mother cried passionately. Everyone she had known there was honest and worked hard. His experiences had been unlucky accidents. Of course it would take time to change society, to educate everyone, but people would learn. In the end it would work. Besides, people in Germany couldn't be that honest, or why was she expected to keep even the linen closets locked? Why did his brothers, who lived in the same house, insist that she, as wife of the eldest, wear a heavy, jangling bunch of keys on her belt like a jailer? Her own family had never locked anything. Not even the front door.

These same exchanges were repeated every so often throughout their married life. Small, incidental things could trigger the cycle – in every house in which they lived, in every subsequent country to which they moved, through endlessly changing world orders. And just as the argument never varied, neither did the stalemate at its end. When it was reached, my father would retire to another room with his books, or get his hat and go for a walk, while my mother went to the kitchen and rattled pots and pans as if they were the culprits.

In the presence of others, my mother was careful not to speak out, gradually learning to make the best of things. This was, after all, her life now. She must have had happy moments too while living in Germany – when she became a mother; when her sisters-in-law did sometimes look up to her; when the family business prospered and a new house was bought, fitted with furniture of her choice. I remember hikes through enchanted forests with frighteningly dark places where no sun filtered through; and picnics in clearings among the trees where my mother always proved quickest at finding wild strawberries or sorrel leaves, their acid puckering our mouths as we chewed them. There were occasions when the whole family went on holiday to this or that spa; or when we took long walks through the countryside, singing together. Glimpses of those walks flash through my mind. Carried on someone's shoulders and named "General Ingemaus" ("maus" being mouse), I would call out commands, "Forward march!" "Turn right!" everyone obeying me but also laughing – though I did command them not to.

My mother enjoyed evenings at the theatre where she became

acquainted first with light operettas, and then with real opera. There was always music. My mother sang a great deal. By the time I was born, she sang as much in German as in Russian, rolling her r's and l's in the same delicious way. She sang whatever she heard on the radio, on records or on the street, everything from fragments of opera to the "Schlager" of the day. I learned to sing them with her, and can still hear Schubert's "Serenade" as I did then, the literal meaning of the words "Lass auch Dir die Brust bewegen", going round and round my head, making me see breasts that moved like arms, beckoning, all important.

The songs sounded tragic or humorous, according to her mood. Sometimes, she seemed perfectly happy but then would begin singing a Russian song and was at once overcome by waves of nostalgia. For her, no singer ever matched the greatness of Chaliapin, no dancer could compare with Pavlova, no poet came anywhere close to Pushkin!

NEW JOURNEYS

Long before it actually materialized, my father could sense the approach of danger. He sensed it in Germany, when my mother was pregnant with me. He would have liked her to board a ship and give birth on the open sea – this, he thought, would open doors for me to different countries in years to come. But my mother had a difficult pregnancy and could not travel, and so, like my older sister, I was born in Germany.

We lived in a comfortable house at No. 10 Humboldtstrasse in Frankfurt. The top floor was occupied by my father's youngest sister, Selma, and her husband Arthur. I loved to climb the steep steps that led up there and knew that as soon as my uncle heard me, he would put one of two operas on his record-player, Verdi's Aïda or La Traviata, then ask me to identify it. With only two choices, my guess was often right and I lapped up his praise. And, oh what excitement there was when my uncle brought home Astor, an Alsatian puppy! From that day forth it became difficult for my mother to tear me away for meals or at bedtime.

My sister's friend, Blümi, lived directly across the road and often came to sit at our window with her where the two girls had long chats. I overheard Blümi ask my sister whether she had bitten my mother's nipples while being breastfed. When my sister said she did not know, Blümi triumphantly boasted, "*I* did! I bit them really hard until they bled and my mother cried! You should have done that too!" Her words horrified me and burned into my mind deeply enough to last a lifetime.

I was proudly walking Astor on a leash up and down in front of our house when Günther, the boy next door who sometimes played with me, came up and said, "I can't play with you any more." "Why?" I asked. "Because you're a Jew", he said.

Dropping Astor's leash, I ran off blindly, straight into a lamppost. My mother must have been watching, because she appeared instantly, retrieved Astor and took me inside. She sat me on the kitchen table and pressed the cold blade of a large knife against the rising bump on my forehead. It took a while for me to stop sobbing though my mother reminded me that I did not want to play with Günther anyway since he had killed my kitten with the iron grid outside our door three weeks earlier. "But what is a Jew?" I asked. I wish I could remember my mother's answer.

Not long after this, when Nazi Storm Troopers burst into my father's business to search the premises, my father sensed that they would soon arrest him on trumped-up charges, as they were doing with other people. He decided there and then that we should leave Germany at once, abandon his business, our house, our German lives. Only safety mattered.

According to a new law we would be stripped of our German nationality upon leaving the country, and become stateless refugees. This meant nothing to my sister and me – she was ten years old and I was not quite four. But to the adults huddled in our kitchen on the eve of our departure, it was part of a larger trauma. Outside the night was black, and everyone spoke in low tones, not at all the way they usually spoke. On other nights, such family get-togethers had been festive. But on this night, the women were crying. Without knowing why, I cried along with them, though my sister did not. When I asked her why we were leaving, she said that it was to get away from bad people. "Like Blümi and Günther?" I wanted to know. She must have said, "Don't be silly!" though even she could hardly have grasped the momentous impact these decisions would have on our lives.

Innumerable people like us were streaming across borders into countries where they were unwanted. Family groups were turned back at the border. It was not safe to travel together or to carry much. Even taking money might have aroused suspicion. My mother had the presence of mind to shop for groceries that day and spread them out on the kitchen table so as to give the impression that all was normal. Then, she thought, should there be a search, it might take longer before anyone realized that the house was truly empty and its occupants on the run. Several of my father's immediate relatives left at more or less the same time. Aunt Selma and uncle Arthur were taking me with them to Belgium. The railway station was crowded, people were pushing and shoving one another, and the chaotic scene was charged with emotion. When Astor, my uncle's dog, suddenly howled pitifully because a guard took him away, his howl spoke for all of us. My aunt quickly lifted me up and I clung to her as she carried me up the carriage steps to our compartment.

Some months later, my mother came to Belgium to fetch me and take me to France, to a large old house in Sèvres that we shared with other aunts, uncles and some cousins. One uncle took us children to see a display of miniature cups and dishes just right for dolls but made of very precious Sèvres porcelain. On our way there and back, he skipped us along and taught us to sing our first French song.

On va bien s'amuser,
on va bien rigoler,
avec les pom-poms, avec les pom-poms,
aaah-vec les pompiers!
We loved it, especially the last refrain.

My father and the other men were trying to find work. My sister was soon enrolled at a nearby school and I at a preschool, where we began to learn French, though of course, at home everyone still spoke German. My sister and I left together in the mornings and on the way, had to pass a house where a ferocious-looking black dog glared at us, barking fiercely. He was chained to his kennel; still, we always held hands at this point. One night my sister dreamt that the dog's chain had come undone and that he charged to attack us. The following morning when we passed the house, the dog really was unchained and with his fierce bark, bounded across the lawn toward us. We ran as fast as we could and, from then on, believed in prescient dreams.

At the end of our year in Sèvres, the family disbanded and moved to Paris. The money they had managed to bring from Germany was fast running out and everyone hoped there would be better opportunities for work in the metropolis.

My parents found a cheap apartment to rent and though their residence permits were only temporary, they felt sure these would be renewed every three months, as had happened since our arrival in France. We did not live in fear, nor in hiding like the "illegal" Algerian street-hawkers we saw. How they ran at the sight of a policeman, with their carts full of wares that often went flying! And compared to those who slept on the street close to foul-smelling métro vents for warmth, we were well-off.

In the apartment, we used wooden boxes for a table and chairs. We slept on the floor but miraculously had pillows. We also had a turtle in the bathtub. It suffered from ticks and my mother removed them with tweezers. But the turtle looked just as sad after the ticks had been removed. It was old, too old to be eaten. At the market no one had wanted it. It looked so forlorn, I begged my mother to let me take it home. She was reluctant, but gave in because turtles, being modest in their wants, only need one leaf of lettuce a day. She liked modesty.

Severe asthma now plagued me and the doctor at the Rothschild Committee's Centre for Refugees recommended that I be sent to a Children's Home in Switzerland. And so, once again, I was put on a train, this time with complete strangers, bound for yet another new destination. It was easy to distract me, and this my mother did at the moment of parting. "Oh, look!" she said, "The lady who is taking care of you is wearing a blouse with red polka dots!" and then she was gone and the train began to move.

Switzerland was an incredible oasis in a world gone mad.

The Children's Home, situated on Mount Rigi, overlooked the Lake of Lucerne. The music of cow bells rang out everywhere on the surrounding slopes. At the Children's Home everyone was kind and cheerful and soon made me feel at ease. On my return to Paris six months later, I was no longer speaking German, but answered all questions in Swiss German instead. Everyone laughed each time I said something, and I was reduced to tears. But when they heard me yodel which I had also learned, we laughed together.

My parents had separate residence permits, and my sister and I were included on my mother's. On the due date, one had to apply person-ally for a renewal. When they went off to do this, we knew that we would not see them for several hours because not only was the Permit Office at some distance by métro, but the waiting room always over-flowed with people. Once my mother had taken us along and we knew the routine. We first gave our name, got a number then sat on benches and waited endlessly for our turn. No one dared nod off or go out to stretch their legs in case their number was called. Each time the door to the inner office opened, all eyes turned to the person who emerged, with the silent question: had he or she been granted asylum for another three months? When despair was written all over their features, we knew. Next to us sat a woman with a baby at her breast and a toddler who would not stop crying. My mother felt sorry for the woman and gave her our number, which was lower. But the officer in charge who, since morning, had watched us and herded us from bench to bench, suddenly announced that no more applications would be considered that day and told everyone to come back the following morning.

The last time our parents went on this errand together and left us alone, my sister was engrossed in her homework but she soon closed her books and said, "Let's jump on the pillows!" She knew it was my favourite game and, though she was six years older, she clearly enjoyed it just as much. She jumped faster and faster and higher and higher on the piled-up pillows, singing "Bella-bella-POUTA-bella!" and on "POUTA ..." poked her puffed up cheeks with a loud popping sound. How we laughed!

Then my sister decided to make a gift for our parents. She made me kneel on a stool and placed our one little lamp next to me so that it would project my silhouette onto a large sheet of packing paper pinned to the wall. On this she tried to draw my outline, but I couldn't keep still and my shadow kept moving. She got impatient and pushed me. I resisted and we had a fight. I remember crying and wishing my mother and father had taken me with them. It was dark outside now. They had left the apartment so long ago. Surely by now that Office would not be open any more. Then why had they not returned? Perhaps permission to stay on in this country had been refused and they were too sad to come home with the news that they – we? – would have to leave. As the hours passed even my sister became nervous. Perhaps our parents had been sent away already, were not even allowed to come back to us. Perhaps they had been put directly on a train to some new destination. There were such cases. We had heard of them.

Or, worse still, perhaps they were forced to take a train back to Germany where Hitler's henchmen would kill them. We often heard Hitler's voice on the little radio my father had bought at the flea market. It had probably come from some restaurant. A coin had to be inserted through a slot to make it start playing. The key for the little coin-drawer was lost and we could use the same coin over and over. As soon as it was inserted, someone spoke, or sang adverts for the oh! so wonderful macaroni, "*Ah, qu'ils sont bons quand ils sont cuits, les macaronis, les macaronis ...*"; or the gentlest, sweetest-smelling soap, "*Mon Savon, Mon Savon, Mon-Sa-a-VON!*"; or a song called, "*Sombre dimanche*" (Black Sunday). Already six people had died by their own hand after listening to "*Sombre dimanche*", the radio announcer said. My sister and I sang the macaroni and soap adverts. We also sang "*Sombre dimanche*" and watched one another carefully to see would one of us die but nothing happened.

During newscasts, snatches of Hitler's speeches were included. When his voice rang out screaming death and destruction, it always made my stomach ache and I had to lie down. My sister's stomach did not hurt. She got angry and left the room. It was not clear to me why she was angry. Perhaps with me? I did not ask her. And once her anger had blown over, I dared not raise the matter again for fear of reactivating it.

But now she was holding me just as tightly as I was holding her. We were standing by the window in the dark, our arms about one another, not daring to switch on the light because it would make us visible from outside. One never knew. We were on the fifth floor, but still. My sister had found a stout stick among the pile of boxes and placed it next to the front door in case we had to hit an intruder. We peered out at the street, hope rising every time a man and a woman turned the corner. If two men turned the corner we glanced back at our front door, making sure the stick was in place. Two men could mean anything. Two men might be from the Permit Office, coming to force us to leave. To put us on a train. To take us to prison. Two men could be Hitler's envoys, sent to kill us. We were both crying by now.

"What will happen to the turtle?" I sobbed. "Silly!" my sister said soberly and, straightening up, wiped away her tears.

Finally, finally our parents came home. "What happened?" we asked, running to them. They looked at one another, then at us. Putting her arms around my sister and me, my mother tried to smile, "We three can stay ..." "And Pappi?" we asked. She shook her head.

My father only hung his. He was ever a silent man. His application had been denied. There was no possibility of an appeal. He would have to leave France. My parents' visible sense of defeat frightened me, and although my sister did not show it, she must surely also have worried about what awaited us next.

We had been fortunate so far. Why a renewal of my father's permit was suddenly refused, remained a mystery. He at once applied for a visa to England and luckily it was granted although it too was only valid for three months. There was no knowing whether this would be extended, therefore he could not take us with him. Our goodbyes were emotional and my mother trembled when he embraced us. We did not know then that we would not see him again for five whole years.

My mother put on a brave face and, for a while, life went on as before. But soon the little money that was left, ran out. She had to give up the apartment, could not even buy food and was forced to apply for help to the Rothschild Committee for Refugees. Although she hated charity with a passion, she now became entirely dependent on it. The Committee arranged to pay the rent for a small room in a cheap hotel, as well as providing courses in millinery and glove-making. At the completion of the courses, the Committee found clients for the "graduates", fully aware that they had no work permits. But what else was one to do? Still my mother's meagre earnings were barely enough to feed her. The price of a métro ticket was often beyond her means, so she walked to her clients. There was no alternative but to let the Committee send my sister and me to a Children's Home. They chose one in Chatenay-Malabry, now considered a suburb of Paris. But in those years there was no métro connection to this area, only an ordinary train and it was expensive. Besides, visits were not encouraged so my mother hardly ever made that journey during the next four years.

At the Children's Home everyone was assigned duties. My sister, being older, had to work much more. Consequently, she and I had little contact with one another. After about one year, she was suddenly sent to another town as "home help" to someone. I did not know why and was told nothing more. We were not even given a chance to say goodbye to one another, but this did not alarm me unduly. I somehow thought it was a temporary arrangement and that she would soon come back. I did miss her, missed knowing her to be close by but such is a child's ability to adapt that I soon accepted the situation, having by then become used to the other children and to the routine. Also, an older boy took me under his wing and so I did not feel alone. His face is still indelibly etched on my memory although it is eighty years since I last saw him. After we were parted, I wrote him many letters but had no address and could not send them. In the end, I only wrote them in my head and still do so at times.

LETTER TO JEAN

I called you Jean and that is how I still think of you. You had told me straight away that your name was really Hans Ernst, but had been changed to Jean-Erneste now that you were in France. Why did you feel you had to tell me this? It would not have occurred to me to question it. I could never question anyone; it was not something that I did. Besides, I was the new arrival, three years younger than you and in my eyes you were practically a grown-up. What drew us together? All I know is that somehow, from the first, a bond formed between us and soon you became central to my life.

The other Hans, who ran the Children's Home, was broad-shouldered and muscular, as you will well remember. He stood tall and with his longish hair combed straight back from a high forehead, I always thought he had the look of an artist or a circus acrobat especially when he wore his black beret pulled well to one side. His name was Hans Joachim, or so he said. We did not quite believe him. If it really was his name, why had he not changed it to something French? He told us to call him Hans and so we did, at least to his face. But after we had seen the initials H. J. carved on a suitcase in the attic, we called him Hitler Jugend behind his back. In his presence we were all puppets. His eyes punctured the hardiest self-confidence and the invisible strings he threaded through us were almost palpable.

Our only refuge was the Hill, "our" Hill. It felt like a stronghold. Up there it was as if his hand couldn't reach us. We built a secret treehouse there, securing a branch here and there and dreamed short dreams whenever we managed to go that far without being missed. At thirteen you were the eldest and the biggest of the children, and you let me help you, even though I was a girl. Did you only pretend not to know that I was every bit as scared as the other girls whom you called silly?

I was scared of the dark, creaking forest and scared of the deserted, sun-baked plateau at the top, where silent snakes slithered behind boulders and watched us. But when you were close by it was alright. There was something special about you, a gentle solidity. Though once, when a snake suddenly barred my path, all the gentleness went out of you as you turned on it with powerful whacks of your stick.

Every so often I felt I had to justify my being with you. I had seen you boys compare the size of your biceps, so I peeled back my sleeve, slowly raised my clenched fist and said, "Look!" If you thought me ridiculous, you never said so, and the others dared not laugh at me in your presence. You called me your pal.

I was also scared when we raided the apple orchards and straw-berry fields, although Hans was right there with us, organizing the whole operation like a military manoeuvre. The raids were his idea. He claimed he could not afford to buy any fruit on the amount he was paid for our keep. We stole the fruit by the bagful with no thought of right or wrong. We stole it because he said we should and we never questioned his orders. But he must have read the fear in my eyes, because once he raised his huge hand above me; then, instead of striking me, he patted me and said, "You're a good girl!" I never knew whether it was a sneer or a joke.

The day he sent us off to steal apples without him, it was very hot. The old broken pram we always took along for the fruit seemed heavier. Red poppies were scattered on the green expanse around us like blood drops. What made us climb the steep incline above the orchards? And someone had the bright idea of pulling the pram up there too. When we got to the top, Roger started fooling around with it, then got into it and rode down the hill. He managed to stay inside it until it reached an abrupt halt at the bottom. After he had pulled it to the top again, you said you would have a go. As soon as you got in, it went off like a wild animal running for its life, hopping when it hit stones, turning this way and that, teetering. You tried to steer it by throwing your weight to one side, then the other, but you had no control whatever, and we stood paralyzed with horror and watched. Faster and faster you went, at an incredible angle. The few seconds it took were like hours. Then the pram hit the tree. You were thrown out, your leg speared by a branch that had snapped off. Your blood was everywhere like scattered poppy petals. Surprisingly, the pram had survived. You were so much bigger than we were, how did we ever lift you back into it and wheel you back to the Children's Home.

We all pushed the pram, going as fast as we could. It squealed like an animal being slaughtered. I didn't want to look at your leg, but my eyes were constantly drawn back to it. The branch was still in it and two ends stuck out like horrible new-grown horns that had bloodily pushed their way through. You didn't cry or moan or say a word. That would have made it easier to bear – for me. You just sat awkwardly in that ridiculous contraption, your legs and arms all over the place, the blood turning a funny dark colour that no longer looked like blood but like the sap of some tree. Your profile, your dear familiar profile, was sagging and suddenly frightening. Were you going to die?

I wanted you to say something, anything. But you didn't and neither did we. As we neared the house, the same thoughts must have been racing round in all our heads: what excuses could we make? What reason could we give for the accident that would make it look blameless? Would you, at least, escape punishment since you were already hurt?

You never cried or protested when you got a beating. Once, on the cellar stairs, you tried to stop him by pleading your innocence, only because you'd caught sight of me at the top. But we both knew he never accepted anyone's word. He was standing several steps above you and was lashing out at you with a broom. You were trying to protect your head with your hands. Though I'd felt sick when I'd seen him hit others, it was nothing compared to what I felt now that he was hitting you. His hair was flying about and what I could see of his face was a purplish red. I'd always thought of you as tall and strong, and suddenly you were neither and I didn't know what to do.

Afterwards, you wouldn't let me bathe your bruises, not even the nasty one above your eye. You simply kept saying you were okay, and I didn't insist because I understood about pride, even though I wasn't a boy. To my "Why? Why did he do it?" you shrugged. "He's crazy ... Says the furnace went out because I didn't clean it yesterday. But I did." Looking after the furnace was one of your many chores. We each had our own.

You couldn't go to school while your leg was healing. You'd hobble up on to the garage roof and sit on a deckchair, your leg stretched out in front of you. It was up there we always had our after-school snack. I ran up to you before any of the others could, and sat down near you. You wore a worn-out pair of shorts in the heat and once they didn't cover the essentials. "There's something slipping out," I said, nodding in that direction, and you re-arranged your shorts. I couldn't have said that to anyone else and I knew you felt the same.

When Gérard was expelled, or "thrown out" as Hans called it, it was you who explained the reason to me. I knew he had sometimes stayed in the toilet longer than anyone else, and I thought that was the reason he was sent away, since there were usually fifteen or sixteen of us and there was only one toilet. But you said it wasn't because he stayed in there; it was what he did in there. "What?" I asked. You looked uncomfortable. "Squeezed out his seeds," you said. That took me by surprise. I pictured little brown seeds like apple pips popping out of him, and I couldn't really see why that was bad, but I gathered from your tone that it was.

After the others joined us, you never said much. We munched the apples we were given for the "quatre-heure" as the after-school snack was called or, when they were too rotten, we threw them into the garden next door. One day the neighbour came over and complained about all the rotten apples piling up in her garden. Hans immediately called us together and his hand outdid itself and seemed to grow with each blow it landed. The next morning the neighbour was waiting for us outside the gate when we left for school. She held her face in her hands and kept repeating, "I saw what he did from my window ... I should never have told him! Never!" But we had to rush off or we'd have been punished at school for being late. We didn't have time for regrets – hers or anyone else's.

Hanna, Hans' wife, was a shadowy figure. She didn't really impinge on our lives. She only helped occasionally with the youngest children, and at times gave Hans a hand in the kitchen. In effect, he ran the whole place single-handedly with whatever help he got from us. He seemed to keep Hanna as a sort of prize to enjoy in their room in the evenings. We weren't allowed across their threshold and never actually saw anything, but there was always some child who made a smutty remark. No doubt, this was prompted by bath night.

Once a week we were shooed into the bathroom, the tub was filled and two or three of us at a time had a bath. Boys and girls were kept separate. When we'd all had our turns, Hans and Anna went in together. They stayed inside a very long time, laughing and splashing and saying things to one another that no one outside ever caught. Still, it caused a lot of nudging, sign language and suppressed giggling, but you, Jean, never took part in it.

There was his hand and there was yours. I liked yours. I liked to watch you make catapults and whistles out of broken branches, or build a fire on the plateau. It didn't matter that you were not a good student, that you were three years older than I but only one grade ahead of me. I was happy to struggle with your homework while your hand was busy turning the potato we'd found and put into the hot ashes of our fire. I was happy knowing you'd cut that potato into two halves. Your hand was special and it was always the same. I would have known it anywhere, among a hundred other hands.

But his hand kept changing. In the wash-house, red and swollen, it was the jaw of a vice that wrung and twisted the water out of the sheets and clothes; on some mornings it was a hard, unforgiving rod that laid into Lydia for wetting her bed; it became an iron ring when, during his gymnastics binges, he swung himself around the bar he'd set up in the yard.

It could also wield a paintbrush. On a good day, he'd sit us round the table he'd set up in the garage and show us how to draw cartoons with a few deft strokes. I tried to do what he was doing, but all that ever appeared on my paper was a group of indistinct figures huddling miserably at the bottom of the page, while, above them, hovered a big hand. When Hans saw it, he slapped his thigh and guffawed, "The hand of God!"

One night, when I was getting undressed, his hand shot out from under my bed and gripped my ankle. The shock robbed me of my voice and I couldn't laugh as I was supposed to, not even that sobbing kind of laughter. But his guffaw filled the silence to bursting. You were in the boy's bedroom, so you didn't see what happened. But you heard the other girls talk about it next morning, and asked me to tell you exactly what had occurred. When I did, a strange look came into your eyes that I didn't recognize. "Were your clothes already off?" you asked. The tone of your unexpected question and that odd expression on your face made me nervous. I got confused and said, "No ... Yes. I mean, some." At this, you stalked off without another word. Then on the way to school, you didn't pay any attention to the rest of us, but kept whacking all the bushes we passed with your stick, as if they were enemies you were fending off. I didn't know what was going on in your mind, but was very relieved when you seemed to have forgotten the incident a couple of days later.

My chores consisted mostly of helping with the youngest children, before school, during the hurried lunch-hour and at bedtime. Mornings and evenings I had to put them on their potties. Several were enameled and one large one was of earthenware. This had to be kept for Julia whose bottom was too big to fit on the others. It was difficult to make the children stay on their potties until they'd done their business but it was up to me to keep them there. They had become adept at moving around with their potties under them by stretching their legs forward and then sliding along on the potty. Of course, there were accidents – the contents of potties splashing out or, worse, spilling completely. To prevent the children from moving, I put belts or ropes around their waists and tied them to the radiator or whatever was behind them. When I finally released them, they had big red rings on their bottoms.

I hated having to wipe them, especially Julia, perhaps because of her size. But with two-year old Peter I didn't mind. He never disgusted me. The way his big blue eyes looked up at me made up for everything. And he was always so happy! What did he have to be so happy about? Even the red ring on his bottom was a smile. Lisa, his four-year old sister, never smiled. She sat in a corner and sang, but it wasn't really singing. It was a sort of wail punctuated by quickly indrawn breath. She mixed up the words of "Au clair de la lune" and "Auprès de ma blonde," and it all came out as a jumble, "Auvé-èche-blonde-lanalune." She repeated this over and over, her eyes disappearing and reappearing like little furtive mice. Neither Lisa nor Peter remembered their parents, who had left them in the Home to go and fight in the Spanish war against Franco. We knew about the war, but not the ins and outs of it. We heard people blaming everything bad on it, but no one ever explained anything.

New children came and went. Most of those who suddenly disappeared, Hans claimed to have "thrown out", ostensibly for "dishonesty" which, in his book, covered an endless variety of misdemeanours, though we never learned any details. These dark, veiled accusations helped to keep us in line. Sometimes, up on our Hill, far from the Home, we whispered our suspicions to one another. We knew that a charitable organization paid for many of us, but we had no idea whether the payments were generous or punctual. Did Hans spirit away the children during the night, if their keep wasn't paid up? Did he drag them miles into the woods and tie them to a tree just as he had done with the dog he suddenly no longer wanted? For weeks and weeks I was sure I could hear him howl and whimper, though you said he must have been dead long since.

By what good or bad fortune you and I were not "thrown out" for a period of years remained a mystery. It made us ever-watchful, not for ourselves but for each other. The possibility that one of us might be left there without the other didn't bear thinking about.

Whenever you were sent to the village Co-op to buy groceries, you always asked, "Can I take someone with me?" Everyone knew I was that "someone." And Hans wasn't always mean about letting us be together, though there was hell to pay the day we lost the grocery money. You must have dropped it because of the mole you'd caught. Its rear end was sticking out of a hole in the ground and, quick as lightning, you got hold of it. You put it down on the path and it ran blindly in circles like a wind-up toy. How we laughed! And then you ran ahead to tease me and I tried to catch you and it was terribly hot, so we rolled on the grass to cool off and disturbed all the bumble bees feeding on the clover. We listened to their warm buzzing and watched the jerky flight of dragonflies, whose shiny bodies were stabbed by the sun. The air was heavy and heady. Suddenly you realized you didn't have the money any more! We searched desperately, combing the grass, retracing our every step over and over, afraid to go home, afraid of being late, which we certainly already were, and finally making the agonizing decision to go back and confess, feeling at the same time that we ought to run, yet not wanting to take another step in that direction. I was terrified. And it was you who'd get the beating! You didn't admit you were afraid, but I saw how your face was set and I could feel the clenching of your teeth as if they were in my own jaw.

Afterwards, when it was all over, you emerged squeezing your sore, swollen hands in your armpits, looking triumphant as you said, "He didn't say I couldn't take you with me any more!"

There was that weekend when the ladies from the charity that funded us were coming to visit. We had to scrub the house and everything in sight, including ourselves. We'd never seen Hans so jittery. He checked and rechecked all our work and was even more critical of it than usual. He gave us all haircuts and though we sat quite still, he complained that we did not, and kept nicking us with the scissors. He sent us to the Co-op to buy groceries we'd never bought before, and after we brought them home he ran off himself and bought some more.

Hanna put on her prettiest dress and set the big table for supper. We were amazed. We'd never had the table set for us; we'd each always carried our own cutlery and plate from the kitchen where Hans ladled out whatever he'd cooked – often food on which we gagged. There'd been many scenes at mealtimes, when the youngest ones held their lips tightly closed, refusing the food, and Hans and Anna pinched their noses to force open their mouths and shoved in the spoons. Hans wasn't going to let good food be wasted, he shouted.

But on this special day, everything looked delicious. There was a place setting for each one of us, and in front of each stood a little pot of yogurt, a delicacy none of us had ever tasted. There was real white bread in the center of the table, and a dish with butter, and cheeses and jams. We'd never been given any of those before. We ran back and forth in front of the open dining-room door, unable to believe our eyes.

When the visitors were due to arrive, we were sent out to the "play-room" – the old garage that Hans had whitewashed the week before.

He'd even painted some of his cartoons on the walls. Through a little side-window, we watched the ladies being ceremoniously admitted at the gate and ushered into the house, but not before Hans had proudly pointed out the big trees to them. What would the ladies have said had they known that he'd punished eleven-year-old Henry by tying him to one of the highest branches of those trees, knowing that Henry was afraid of heights. We'd never come this close to the "top brass" and there were so many things we'd promised ourselves to report if we ever got the chance.

Now, while the ladies were given a tour of the superb supper table, then taken into Hans and Hanna's private room and offered tea with little dainty things, we stood in the garage and counted up our grievances. We couldn't possibly mention them all. Right, then only the most serious ones. But which were more serious than others? The beatings? The "throwing out" of children? The carefully calculated punishments? The food? The unfairness of it all! Somehow we *had* to tell. Tell all we could. For everyone's sake. No matter what the consequences. And so it went, until Hanna and Hans brought the ladies out to have a peek at us and bestow a gracious smile. Hans, in carefully pressed white trousers, beamed, turning us back into dumb puppets. Then he put one hand on your shoulder and one on mine and said to the ladies, "These two are our prize children!" The ladies oohed and aahed and said that everything was most satisfactory, and then they left.

No sooner had the gate clicked to behind them, than Hans and Hanna dashed into the house. By the time we got back inside, everything had been whipped off the dining-room table. There was no white bread or butter, no jam or yogurt. Even the place settings were gone. It was as if the whole thing had been a mirage.

Hanna complained of being exhausted and went off to lie down. Hans dished up the usual stew in the usual way. The mood was a grey shroud hanging over us. No one spoke. After the others had gone upstairs, you went down to the cellar to do some of your chores.

I lingered in the dining-room, staring out of the window. "Pssst!" Hans said from the hall and motioned me to come to the kitchen. What had I done wrong this time? He always made a mystery of it until the last possible moment, and then hurled the accusation at us like a grenade.

I stepped into the kitchen as if it were a fiery furnace. "C'mon! C'mon!" Hans urged, "I have something for you!" *His* kind of humour, I thought. He was going to give me a slap ... But no! He was holding out one of the little pots of yogurt. To me! I was stunned. "Mustn't let the others see!" he said in a stage whisper and closed the kitchen door.

He grinned, "Aren't you going to say anything?"

I just stared, sure it was some kind of trick. "Cat got your tongue? Let's see!" He took my face in his hands and opened my mouth. "Ah! There it is! I can see it!" He tickled me. First under my arms. It wasn't a bit funny, but I laughed. I didn't want to, but it was as if he were pressing a button. "There! That's more like it!" he said and tickled me harder, till I doubled over and held my sides. "A ticklish miss, eh?" he went on, his big hands now pincers. I sank to the floor. The pincers slid under my skirt and worked their way up my thighs. I wanted to scream, but instead kept laughing that horrible laugh, tears rolling down my cheeks. His big grin loomed above me and his eyes were glassy as if there was no one behind them. And I knew that, even if I could have talked, it wouldn't have made any difference. It was his hand that was in control. Of him too.

When you burst into the kitchen, his hand was hurting me and the sounds coming out of me could no longer be mistaken for laughter. The instant he saw you, he sprang up from the floor. He looked wild and screamed, "I won't put up with you any more! You're both liars! I'm throwing you out! Both of you! I want you gone tomorrow!"

I lay awake all night and I know you must have, too. I kept wondering, was I a liar? What had I lied about? I never found out. We were packed off very early the next morning. On different trains. He must have done that on purpose. I didn't find out where yours was taking you. I hardly dared look straight at you and was left with a blurry impression of blood-shot eyes in a grimly set face. Your hair was dishevelled. Mine must have been, too. We'd been hustled out of the house before the others were up.

Years later I still looked for you. I looked everywhere, even in places where I had no reason to believe you might be. Once, from a moving bus, I was sure that I saw you. The driver cursed me as I jumped off to search the streets. And once I heard your special whistle outside, the one we used as a signal. I threw open the window but you weren't there.

Are you still somewhere, Jean?

AH, MON PARIS!

My father and mother exchanged frequent, lengthy letters, and he sent her what little money he could. But only after four years was he able to supplement her tiny income in a substantial way. Very fortunately, this happened to coincide with my departure from the Children's Home. Now that my mother could suddenly afford to have us live with her, my sister, too, could come back.

No country wanted to be burdened with refugees and England was no exception. When my father's English visa had expired at the end of three months, he had been forced to leave that country, just as he had had to leave France. The only thing possible for him was to go further west, to Ireland where, very fortunately, he could stay. But because he was penniless, he was not allowed to let his family join him. Permission to do so would only be given when he could prove that he earned enough to support us. He looked for work, sold ties from door to door, and took any job he could find, but Ireland was very poor at that time and prospects were few. Still, it was not his way to give up. The thought of us in Paris sustained him. He struggled on and now, four years later, was at last able to send money to my mother regularly.

How good it was to feel my mother's arms around me, to be close to her again! Though I was older, there was no estrangement between us. She was still my mother. However, I was not myself. Plagued by nightmares, sleeping only fitfully, I often woke up screaming, which left me tired and listless during the day. The Rothschild Committee's doctor could find no plausible physical explanation. My mother did her best to pry out of me what was wrong. Had something occurred at the Home that was upsetting me? But I was unable to speak about it, could not find the words to formulate an answer.

It was different when I was with my sister. She knew. She had been there and needed no explanation. When she and I were alone, we sometimes referred to what we had seen and some of what we had lived through, and we both swore that we would report everything to some authority. But curiously, neither she nor I ever whispered a word about it to any other person, and certainly not to my mother. Perhaps especially not to my mother, whom we did not want to hurt or upset. And would anyone else have believed us? My sister never confided to me exactly why she had suddenly been sent elsewhere at the end of our first year, while I remained there for another three. She got extremely angry when I put the question to her and never spoke of it to me or to anyone else as long as she lived. But in truth, there was no real need for her to tell me anything. I had a visceral sense of it that needed no words.

My mother's tiny room, rented by the month, felt like home at once, simply because she was there. She herself lived only for the day when we would be able to rejoin my father, while for us, after our four years away, being with her in that room was sheer bliss! The shiny black plaque next to the hotel entrance said, "Hôtel de Bretagne" and underneath the name it promised "Tout comfort". No one else, not even my sister, agreed, but in my eyes living there was the height of luxury. It did not even seem bad to me that our room was fumigated every so often to rid it of bed lice – this was an ongoing battle since they came back through the wall as soon as the room next to ours was fumigated. We learned to accept fleas and lice as part of existence. My mother became quite expert at catching them between her thumb and index finger, then drowning them in a glass of water.

The Hôtel de Bretagne was situated on the Rue des Trois Bornes, and our room was up three flights on a circular staircase. We had a stone sink with cold running water, and a small gas ring to cook on. The wooden "head" on which my mother stretched felt caps for the hats she made, stood on the only table. There were also soft goatskins for gloves. My sister attended the Lycée Jules Ferry some distance away, but the Ecole de Jeunes Filles where I went, was immediately across the street. My mother could wave to me from her window when I came out of the big doorway at 4 o'clock. Sometimes we would take the métro to the Parc Monsouris or the Parc Monceau, where she would settle on a bench in the shade and do some mending she had brought along, while I ran off here and there to "explore". Once, in a clearing, I saw a black man dressed in exotic, colourful robes striding back and forth and calling out forcefully, "Je suis Roi! Roi du Centre de la Terre! Oui! Du Centre de la Terre!" He was tall, handsome and imposing enough to be a king. What did he mean by the Centre of the Earth? And why was he here, unattended? Had he been overthrown? This was a fate that had befallen many kings according to our history books. Could a king be a refugee? I ran off to get my mother, but when we returned, he had gone.

Most of the people staying at the same hotel were from other countries, and they too were waiting, hoping, praying for visas to brighter horizons, to South Africa, to America. The proprietors, Monsieur B. and his wife, were a kind couple. They ran a bar/bistro downstairs and once, to my delight, allowed me to help polish the glasses. It was a celebration of sorts. On that day there had been a "raffle", the French word for a police raid. This happened at irregular intervals. They came to check on everyone's residence status and to uncover anyone working without a permit. Whenever the police came, usually in twos, the proprietors tried to warn at least one of us to alert the others. This time Madame B. had given the signal to Lisbeth, a photographer who had a room on the first floor. She threw her cameras under her bed, then ran up the stairs knocking on doors, calling hoarsely, "Les flics sont là!" The Polish tailor, Monsieur Hinnerang, quickly hid the suit he was working on – though he did forget to remove the tape measure hanging round his neck. Frau Lederer, who had come from Vienna only a few weeks earlier with her young son, had not yet found work and was in no danger, nor was Francis, the painter on the 2nd floor. No one could prove that he was selling any paintings, and he rarely did, but his partner, Manya, made hats, like my mother, and had to be warned. My mother, with her keen antennae, had at once guessed what was happening and had already hidden all telltale signs of her work by the time Lisbeth reached our floor.

The policemen climbed all the way to the top floor, knocking on doors at random. Did they know that we stood behind them with bated breath, listening to their every step? The inspection went without a hitch. Since they neglected to look on top of wardrobes, under beds or under bedcovers, everyone was saved. They did linger in José's attic room. José was a journalist who worked for a Spanish newspaper opposing the Fascists in Franco's Spain. He had gone out that day, leaving his typewriter in full view. But nothing incriminating was found. The Spanish civil war was raging at that time. José had participated in it and lost an arm, but then managed to escape to France. He continued to be passionately anti-fascist, and we often heard him pounding his typewriter throughout the night with his remaining hand. In between writing articles, he painted the walls in the Hotel – in lieu of paying rent.

José came in late for the celebration. He looked even more care-worn than usual. The situation in Spain was worsening, he said. Franco's Nationalists were merciless in their tactics against the "Free Spanish" whose situation was desperate. It was impossible to say how much longer they could hold out.

Monsieur B. calmly declared that in France everyone was perfectly safe. He ended by saying, "No one can touch us here." Francis, the painter, shook his head. He was German, but he too had fought against the Fascists in Spain with the International Brigade of volunteers. When his branch of the Brigade was routed, he had returned to Paris. "One can't be sure of anything!" he said. "The Germans are arming them-selves to the teeth!" But Madame B. cried, "You're forgetting the Maginot Line! It's so well reinforced that no army, absolutely no one from outside, can ever cross it!" Lisbeth, the photographer, swearing as usual, said, "They b--- better not!" Madame B. insisted, "The Maginot Line is impenetrable! They'll never even cross this much of it!" and she clicked her thumbnail against a front tooth to illustrate how little. Then she declared firmly, "There'll never be another war!"

Among French people there was widespread confidence in the Maginot Line, which was then being built against a possible German invasion. It was described as the "strongest fortification ever undertaken". Newspapers published photographs of soldiers stationed there, posing with society ladies who had provided rose-bushes for them to plant alongside the barrier.

Less than a year later, Franco's troops were so successful that most surviving volunteer fighters left Spain. They returned and dragged themselves slowly and painfully across Paris. Francis took me to wave to them as they passed, a line of dejected men of all ages, some on crutches with limbs missing, some with wounded heads or limbs partly covered in dirty bandages. "Did no women come back?" I asked, thinking about Lisa and Peter in the Children's Home, whose parents had both gone to join the International Brigade of volunteers in Spain. I remembered how sad little Lisa's songs sounded, more like sobbing than singing. Were she and Peter orphans now? "Not many women went to fight in Spain", Francis answered, trying to reassure me. "I know of one," I murmured, but he did not hear me.

These broken men, at the end of their strength, whom we watched making their painful way through the Paris streets, looked exactly like those Francis had painted on some of the canvasses in his room, recreating scenes he had himself witnessed in Spain. One canvas in particular that showed a hollow-faced woman offering her limp breast to a dying man, haunted me for years.

It was a very sad day. Our hearts went out to those defeated people. My sister was of course better able to understand these events than I, but neither one of us grasped the larger implications of what had come to pass. For the present it had no tangible impact on our lives. We were happy, happy to be with my mother, happy at school, happy in Paris – our *"Centre de la Terre"!*

THE KING'S VISIT

Everyone was taken by surprise the day Mademoiselle Lemaçon, the Directrice, came into our classroom to announce that the King and Queen of England were coming to Paris on a state visit. Then, lowering her voice, she conferred with Mademoiselle Dupeux, who cast an eye across the rows of girls and, to our astonishment, called out Colette's name and mine, that is, the name she had given me, Angèle. (She had felt sorry for me when the other children, unable to pronounce my name, added an "S" – turning it into the French word for monkey, "singe".) Colette and I were to go to meet the King! Two children from every classroom in the school would go to wave one French flag and one English one at the Royal party. Why had we two been chosen? We never found out. But everyone else looked at us with deep envy.

Long after the Directrice had left the room, her words hung in the air. The clock's hands seemed to stand still. We would have to dress in white, Mademoiselle Dupeux had stressed. Oh, how lucky that I had somehow acquired a white dress! And I did have white socks, but my shoes … Would my mother be able to whiten them?

When we were finally liberated, I sprinted across the street to the Hôtel de Bretagne, looking up to see whether my mother was at our window watching out for me. But on that day she was not. Climbing the circular staircase two steps at a time I almost bumped into José who stood on a ladder, painting the walls. "Eh, là!" he called. "Doucement, la petite!" Mumbling "Pardon!" I rushed past him into our room and, all in one breath, burst out with my news! My mother couldn't believe it either. She had been stretching felt for the hats she made and let everything slip from her hands. "May I go and tell Francis?" I asked, but without waiting for a reply, I was already rushing back down to the floor below. Her voice followed me, "Knock on the door first!"

Blushing, I remembered the last time when, bursting with news, I had *not* knocked. Thanks to Francis who had helped me, I had won a competition for compiling the longest possible list of painters, and I could not wait to show him my prize: a biography of Nostradamus. Rushing down to the room he shared with Manya, I threw the door open... and Francis jumped. He had been bending over a completely naked young woman on the bed. He who had always been my friend, suddenly seemed angry with me. As for me, I felt prickly all over and instantly disliked the intruding young woman. (She was a model, he explained to me later). Manya was not there.

This time I knocked and Manya's voice called out, "Come in!" As in our room, felts, ribbons and feathers from her millinery work trailed everywhere. The paintings that Francis never sold, many depicting scenes from the Spanish Civil War, leaned against the walls.

Manya looked at me with her large dark eyes and explained that Francis had found work. As much as he could handle! For everyone! English and French paper flags to be glued on to wooden sticks, she said, but she did not know their purpose. "For the King!" I told her, "He's coming. To Paris!"

When the others in the hotel heard about the work they were jubilant. This included José, the Spanish journalist; Lisbeth, a buxom woman incapable of opening her mouth without swearing – she even stuck large reminders on her walls saying, "HALT'S MAUL!" ("SHUT YOUR TRAP!"); and Mr. and Mrs. Hinnerang, whose younger son, Jarek, a nice boy of twenty, sadly deformed and no taller than I, was in love with my sister. Jarek never uttered a sound in her presence, nor did he dare look straight at her. But I often caught him gazing at her adoringly when her head was turned away. His older brother, Adek, a medical student, was our "doctor in the house". Tall and handsome, the darling of all the women, he had several lady "patients". I, however, was afraid of him since he'd burned my chest with cupping-glasses – a favourite treatment for coughs.

All these people were waiting, just as we were, as thousands were, for visas to other countries, to South Africa, to America. Any country would do, so long as one might find acceptance and a work permit there. And while waiting, one had to live, earn a few centimes, no matter how, no matter where.

We children were aware that the adults suffered from being foreigners, from floating in limbo. They worried about the future. But to us the future was a nebulous abstraction. So long as we behaved like our classmates, the present was quite concrete. Paris became our city, France our country. Even Fritz, Frau Lederer's little boy, had begun to adapt and no longer chalked "Für Juden verboten"("Forbidden to Jews") on street benches, copying what he had seen in Vienna.

Soon the papers were full of the planned itineraries for the Royal party. There were detailed menus of the meals they would be offered, and lengthy descriptions of the 365 outfits made by France's best couturiers for two life-size dolls – one for each Princess. All this caused much discontent and grumbling among the poorer working-class people with whom we mixed, who were shocked at the extravagance, at their hard-earned taxes being spent on these idle visitors instead of on poor and needy citizens. Refugees did not share these sentiments, we could not relate to them. But I did wonder at the choice of gifts, knowing that Princess Elizabeth was older than I, and I certainly no longer played with dolls. Surely she did not either?

When Francis came back laden with packages of paper flags and wooden sticks, there was a great to-do. My mother placed a pot of glue in the centre of our round table and everyone crowded around it and went to work, anxious to get as many flags done as quickly as possible. I ran back and forth with Francis to deliver the finished flags and get more to work on. Someone asked, was I really going to see the King? "Yes," my mother assured them, "She's going to wave two little flags…" This caused a stir. Perhaps I'd be holding two of the very flags they were assembling! Then why not keep two for me? Why not indeed. Suddenly an idea began to form. At that time (up until 1948) Ireland was a member of the commonwealth, and therefore under the King's jurisdiction. Perhaps we could write a message on one or two of the flags for the King to see. Then he might agree to see me. It would give me the chance to ask him to intercede on our behalf for visas to Ireland!

My imagination was fired. My head spun. Not only was I to meet the King, I had *business* with him! How would I set about it? Did he understand French? For I knew no English. Should I say, "Votre Majesté"? Or "Sire"? I felt terribly hot and left the room, then the hotel. Outside I took great gulps of air, then ran along the street, knocking against people, not seeing anything.

At night I dreamed about it. At school, I was dying to tell my classmates, but I did not. They would no doubt see it in the papers. I only said that we would very soon leave for Ireland. "Oh, where is that?" they asked. When I pointed to it on a map, one of them said, "Sideways it looks like a small terrier barking!" and they all laughed.

The few remaining weeks before the big event passed all too quickly. I would have liked to stretch them out, to have more time for preparation. But the day arrived. The special bus pulled up outside the school at the appointed hour and took us to the Place de la Concorde where we would wait for the Royal party. Apart from the deafening pounding of my heart, I felt empty. I clung to my flags, hiding them as best I could. I would have to unfurl them instead of those they handed to us on the bus. Francis had painted "VIVE LE ROI!" on them in huge letters and underneath, just as large, "HELP ME!" I was ashamed of them. I did not want pity – no more from the King than from anyone else. But how could I ignore this unique opportunity to reunite my parents? Their fate was in my hands.

We were placed in position and repeatedly told to wait for the signal to lift the flags high and wave them. We waited, terribly excited at first, then impatient and finally, little by little, with boredom. Would they never come? Had they missed a turn? At long last the signal was given and the flags went up. Mine would not unfurl properly. In my anxiety I must have wound them too tightly. Struggling with them, I looked around nervously, fearful of being caught. But no one noticed. All eyes were on the shiny black cars gliding by slowly, and everyone waved madly – except for me. Someone asked when would the Royal car come, the one with the King and Queen? "But it just passed!" came the answer. No! That was impossible! "*Mais si!*" The Queen's gloved hand had been in full view! The Queen's ... *hand?* ... In full view? My chest swelled. Sobs shook me. Not only had the King not seen *me;* I was so stupid that I had not seen *him.* How could I face my mother, my sister, our friends ... all of them were expecting to see my photo in the paper. How could I confess that I had botched my mission? Through my tears, everything became a blur.

We piled into our bus, resumed our seats and were soon deposited in front of the school. Slowly I crossed the street and dragged my feet up the hotel stairs. My mother, in her usual seat, looked up when I opened the door and said at once, "The King was too self-important, right?" "No, no! It was all my fault!" I cried and burst into tears, throwing myself into her arms. She stroked my head, "Don't worry, darling! You'll see; everything will be alright!"

"Can't we stay in Paris? All our friends are here ... I don't want to go to Ireland!" I sobbed and added, "Did you see it properly on the map? Sideways, it looks like a little terrier barking!"

DEPARTURE

From the moment we first arrived in France in 1932, we lived in high hopes of making that country our home, though we quickly became aware of the animosity already prevalent against anything or anyone German. It provided a strong motivation for my sister and me to learn the language quickly, to try to lose our foreign accents. Oh, how badly we wanted to be French! If we inadvertently slipped into German and were overheard, there were immediate shouts of "*Sales boches!*" (dirty Huns).

The situation was far more serious in 1937, when my mother was at last able to take us back to Paris to share her small room in the Hôtel de Bretagne. In the distant suburbs where we had stayed in the intervening years, there had been less awareness of world events or headlines. But in Paris, we heard the German threat constantly discussed everywhere, by everyone. There was no escaping it. Although we had had to change schools several times, we no longer felt different from the other children. We imbibed patriotism along with our class-mates, sang the Marseillaise and now, just as they did, instead of singing the official text, we substituted bloodthirsty anti-Nazi rhymes when we were not observed. "*Hachez, hachez les hitlériens, pour en faire du boudin ...*" ("Chop up, chop up, the hitlerites to make blood sausage of them ...")

In our history lessons we learned to revere not only Louis XIV, the Sun King who had ushered in a golden age of art and literature, but also Robespierre whose democratic reforms led to the monarchy's downfall; we identified with Jeanne d'Arc and were deeply affected by her terrible fate at the stake. In literature, we laughed with Molières and loved Victor Hugo; as for scientists like Louis Pasteur and Pierre Curie, we believed their genius to be unequalled in any other country. France had become our spiritual home. In my music class we learned to sing Schubert's song "The Trout". I loved not only its melody, but also the thought of the clever little trout evading the angler's line to glide away to freedom. In my ignorance, I took it for granted that Schubert was French and felt devastated later to learn that he was not.

We wrote loving, cheerful letters to my father telling him what we were learning, describing our classmates and our teachers. My sister had strong feelings about the latter whom she either adored or dismissed as lacking in merit, and she explained all this in great detail to my father. He was our confidant, we wrote and wrote to him, holding back nothing. His replies were usually confined to a sentence or two at the end of his letters to my mother, and our many questions were left unanswered. But we did not hold it against him. My mother had explained how much he wanted to write to us more fully, but that he simply could not. His work kept him terribly busy, and was that not wonderful? He was working very hard for us, to be able to bring us to Ireland where we would be a proper family again. We should feel all the closer to him. "*Mein heiss-geliebter Pappi …*" ("My hotly beloved Daddy …") my sister headed her rapturous letters, still able to write to him in fluent German. Since I had never learned to write German, I did the best I could, writing the German words I knew verbally but using French phonetics.

We had been back with my mother more than a year when the fateful letter from my father arrived, announcing that he was now earning enough to satisfy the requirements of the Irish Government. He had obtained permission for us to join him! He would make travel arrangements for us to leave as soon as possible. "At last, at last!" he wrote, overwhelmed with emotion.

My sister and I were devastated! Leave? But this was where we now belonged! After so long a wait, the dream of joining my father had lost its basis in reality. By this time, deep down, we had no longer believed that it would ever happen. Even our letters to him suddenly seemed like a game we had played. We were inconsolable at the prospect of an imminent departure. In our eyes no other country, whatever it had to offer, could possibly measure up to France.

I ran to the nearby DIMAX on the rue du Faubourg du Temple and bought postcards of the Tour Eiffel and the Arc de Triomphe, desperately looking around to see what else I could take with me that was small enough to pack and also cheap. Some of the vendors at their stalls along the side of the road from whom my mother usually bought vegetables and fruit, now recognized me and called out, "*Bonjour, mon p'tit chou!*" and "*Ta maman n' vient pas aujourd'hui?*" It was all achingly familiar and I would miss every part of it.

To celebrate the visas, my mother took us to the Gaumont, a posh cinema we could never afford before, to see "Mon Paris" a film with Harry Bauer, a revered actor. He played a taxi driver who broke down utterly when forced to leave Paris. At this I burst into uncontrollable sobs. My mother took me outside so as not to disturb other spectators, and we waited in the lobby for my sister. She could not tear herself away until the film ended.

Why we boarded a ship in Dieppe, I never found out. It would have been a much shorter journey to the British coast from Calais, and our crossing of La Manche was ghastly. The storm that raged at sea that day, the worst in years, had my mother convinced that we would never make it to England, would never see my father, would probably not live through it. Like everyone else on board, even some of the crew was violently sick. Trunks, boxes and other large pieces of luggage, that had been neatly stacked against the sides of the deck in Dieppe, now slid freely to and fro on the wet surface, washed by fresh waves every few moments. But no one bothered to secure them, everyone was past caring. Still, we did make it to the other side, where my sister learned that we had crossed not "La Manche", but the "English Channel". She explained this to us, indignantly adding, "It doesn't belong to the English!" This was the attitude she and I adopted from the first, with me of course following her lead, always defending France.

My father had arranged for someone to meet us at the dock and take us to London by train, then help us to transfer to another train to Holyhead on the west coast of Wales. We could never have managed any of this on our own. As we sat with our faces glued to the window, chugging across England, we wondered why every station we passed was called "COLMAN's MUSTARD". Only later did we learn that all geographical names had been removed in case of a German invasion.

With what trepidation my mother must have set off on this journey, every mile bringing her closer to a husband she had not seen for five years. She had endured five interminable years of separation, of longing for this day, always repeating that she hated Paris and could not wait to leave. She blamed French bureaucracy for everything: for having torn her family apart, for being forced to give up her children because, without her husband, she could neither feed nor clothe us; for the terrible loneliness and despair, which often caused her to cry herself to sleep. But we had also seen her laugh in Paris. We had seen her enjoy the company of people who had become good friends. We had heard her sing as she went about her tasks, as she had sung all her life – sad songs sometimes, but happy ones at other times. She must have wondered in what subtle ways her husband might have changed. And whether she herself was still the same person he had left behind.

In the pages and pages he had written her every week, he asked for advice on so many aspects of his life and work: how best to handle those working for him; how to stop the thread in his sewing machines from breaking continually – drawing diagrams to show the exact spot on the machine where it broke. He asked how to carry on when she was so far away, when he was so desperately lonely.

Worn out after her day's work, longing to lie down, she had sat at her little table and answered his every question. She wrote slowly and painstakingly. Writing did not come easily to her. She had done so little of it in her life and never trusted herself to write in any language other than Russian. Did she tell him that she, too, wondered how to keep going? Wondered whether he was finding solace with someone else? He was shy, yes, but even shy men had that terrible male need that drove them. Had he really waited only for her all this time? And how would he see her now? Would he still find her attractive? She was five years older. Already she had begun to find stray grey hairs among the black, which she plucked impatiently as if they were intrusive insects.

During the two days of travel she said little to us. How much apprehension was mixed with her joy at the prospect of a reunion?

In Holyhead we boarded another ship to cross the Irish Sea to Dun Laoghaire. Again the crossing was rough with stiff winds, but it was shorter and less violent than the previous one had been. My sister and I stayed on deck and, clinging to the rail, peered ahead into the unknown. My sister said we should swear to one another that we would return to France very soon, that we would never accept a substitute, even if it meant leaving our parents who, after all, would now have one another. And to seal that solemn promise, she said, we must both spit into the Irish Sea. So we bent over the rails and spat. But a gust of wind carried our saliva back into our faces. We did not see France again for very many years.

At the harbour in Dun Laoghaire, a stranger was waiting for us when we got off the ship. He was our father.

EIRE

In Ireland we felt as if we had been dropped from above into a strange new reality. The closeness to my father that had felt so real as we poured out our hearts to him in letters while we were still in France, completely evaporated in his presence. Now that we were together, we no longer knew how to speak to him and seemed to have nothing to say. He obviously had no clue either about how to bridge the distance between us. He must have expected us to be unchanged, to be the same two little girls he had left behind, whom he could easily amuse. In the past he had only needed to play a recording of canned laughter and we would double over helplessly, giggling until our stomachs ached. Instead, he was now faced with a strong-minded teenager from whom his younger child took her every cue.

My mother could only repeat how very fortunate we were to be a family again, to be with my father after the long years of forced separation. She had sworn that she would never complain, no matter how hard the work might be, if only she got the chance to do it together with him. True to her word, she grasped the challenge of helping him build a new life with her whole being, wasting no time on regrets. But my sister and I continued to long for France, body and soul. In self-defense, we ridiculed everything new and strange to us in Dublin: the open fireplaces that people huddled around to catch a little warmth; the green two-tiered buses that drove on the wrong side of the road; and the Irish accent that my sister could not

Author's 1940 sketch of a Dublin newsboy

understand at first. She had been taught BBC English at school in France, and so could not translate for my mother and me. We desperately missed everything that had become our norm and again swore to one another that we would not stay in Ireland. Yet stay we did, and it became our second love.

Among those members of our family who had remained in France and Belgium, several were deported to concentration camps and some perished there. But we only learned all this at the end of the war, when the full tragedy was revealed. Ireland was a miraculous safe haven. We were incredibly lucky to be there. Gradually we adapted to this new existence, to the English language and to Irish culture, but it took far longer for us to feel a little Irish than it had taken to feel very French. Changing countries now that we were a little older, was more difficult for my sister and me than it had been the first time. Also, among the cosmopolitan population of Paris, we had gone unnoticed once we had learned the language. At our French schools, we had been made to feel part of a nation. Neither held true in Ireland.

Few foreigners had settled there in those years, and this made us conspicuous. In addition, clear divisions existed here between people of different cultural backgrounds and especially of different religions, albeit they were not fed by the deep hatred and bitterness that later festered in the English North of the country. We became very conscious of these demarcation lines that were hardly ever crossed. Once again we were identified as Jews, but in no way did we fit into the small Jewish community. This was especially true of my sister and me, since we had not been brought up in the faith. My parents had never practiced the religion themselves. Though my father firmly believed that religion was necessary to uphold moral standards, he himself was unable to believe. His small factory now occupied his every waking hour, and my mother joined him there whenever possible. Only on rare occasions did either of them take the time to socialize with anyone.

My sister had few opportunities to meet people of her own age and it took a long while for her to find friends. It was easier for me at school, though not before I had learned some English.

All along, there had been much talk about war but it still seemed to be speculation. I understood little of what was happening, although, from the safety of our Dublin vantage point, my family closely followed the news, which was disturbing and confusing. In March of 1938 Hitler's troops marched into Austria and newspapers showed photos of jubilant crowds in Vienna greeting the German Nazis. Also in March, Chamberlain, the British Prime Minister, pledged to defend France and Belgium against "unprovoked aggression", but said Britain would not fight to protect Czechoslovakia. Yet one month later, in April, an Anglo-French pact was signed promising a joint defence of that country should it be attacked. Did this mean there would or would not be open war? It remained unclear.

For his business, my father rented third floor premises in one of the very old buildings that lined Ormond Quay, along the Liffey. Although he had never done any manual work before, he had begun by renting a sewing machine to stitch together sections of handbags for a leather goods manufacturer who showed him how to do it. Once he had mastered this, he rented a second sewing machine and employed a girl to help him, and so on. By the time we arrived in Ireland, my father had become a manufacturer himself, with a staff of ten or so. Since unemployment was rampant, the Irish government encouraged anyone who was able to provide jobs. My father's having done so helped him finally to obtain permission for us to join him.

Having lived in the poor quarters of Paris, we were certainly no strangers to people in rags struggling to survive and beggars squatting on sidewalks. But never before had we encountered anything to equal the squalor and misery of Dublin's poor, so evident in some of the areas we passed on our way to and from my father's place of work. Quite often, drunks – women as well as men – lay on the street and were simply ignored. Since those years, a great opening of doors and windows has taken place, and Ireland's fortunes have changed considerably. But in the early 1940s when we knew it intimately, poverty was rampant there.

After school I often went straight to the factory rather than home to an empty house. Gradually I came to know everyone there. It was fascinating to me to watch the work in progress and the dynamics of the place. Along the streets and bridges across the Liffey that we passed on the way, there were usually beggars sitting on the ground. We gave what we could, where and when we could. One man in particular aroused our curiosity and pity. Rain or shine, he occupied the same spot on the Ha'penny Bridge. His rag of a coat covered his torso. There were no legs and two crutches stood propped up beside him. Naturally we felt particularly sorry for him, wondering why he chose to sit in what must have been the coldest spot on the Liffey, where wrought iron railings provided no shelter against wind or rain. Then, one evening, we left my father's factory later than usual, and as we passed the Ha'penny Bridge, we saw the legless beggar push aside his rags, rise stiffly from the ground on two normal legs, then shuffle off into the gathering dusk, his crutches tucked under one arm. This was a revelation to us and an introduction to the world of Irish beggars. We learned to accept them, even to laugh with them on occasion. For instance the "Friday man", as we called him, came to our door regularly on that day and my mother always gave him three pence. But once, he missed a week and when, on the following Friday, my mother held out the usual coins, he looked at them, then at her and said, "Ah, missus, you owe me sixpence!"

One rainy, windswept night my sister answered the door to a woman holding a very wet, blanketed bundle in her arms, who asked for "something for me poor child". My sister ran to the kitchen for some food and, as she returned to the door, a sudden gust of wind blew open the blanket in the woman's arms. My sister was shocked to see that the "child" was only a big bottle, and said something to that effect. The woman looked at her defiantly and said, "Ah, God forgive you Miss, you wouldn't want me to bring out me poor child on a night like this!"

The people who worked for my father were among the poor and we were aware of their wretched living conditions. We saw tenement houses where, in some cases, an entire family lived in one room with no running water and only a communal toilet down some dark, dank hallway smelling of urine. My mother took me with her once to bring some food to one of the women who was too ill to come to work. The state of the room was dismal and we were dismayed to see four small children all bundled into the only bed. Where did the parents sleep, we wondered.

Another time, we took some Christmas cheer to a young mother who, because of a sick child, could not come to the party that my mother had made for the entire staff at the factory. Again we were struck by the squalor we found, and by what unhealthy lives many people here led. We learned that, among other illnesses, cases of tuberculosis were far from uncommon, though some also occurred among the less poor. Two people in our small circle of acquaintances were stricken with it, as was a neighbour across the street from us. No local treatment was available at that time. There were only hospices for the dying. Some of the wealthier people who could afford it, traveled to Switzerland to stay in sanatoria, though not during the war, when travel was impossible. At some point, I became infected with TB myself but it was only discovered many years later when it suddenly flowered.

The Christmas party became a yearly tradition that my mother organized. My father, being his shy, withdrawn self, rarely speaking unless spoken to, had never been able to do such things while on his own. He would not have known where to begin. I gradually began to understand – though perhaps never quite grasping this while he was alive – that my father had always been a stranger everywhere, struggling to fit in. Although my mother was at first unable to communicate verbally, she somehow managed with simple gestures and expressions, to establish a personal relationship with the workers. The boys whom my father had taught to become leather cutters – first having had to learn how to do it himself – were also his delivery boys. They tended to be shy and rather private. But the girls and women soon opened up to my mother. Since she spent such a large part of the day in their company, it was from them that she picked up her first words of English, "pliers", "scissors" etc. And soon, thanks to her quick ear, she learned enough to converse with them, albeit haltingly.

My father strove for acceptance through conformity, but this was a country whose history is an epic of rebellion. Without my mother he was lost. She was his anchor. Unlike him, she quickly fitted in anywhere in a completely natural way, without any conscious effort.

Always on the lookout for ways to make their work pleasanter and at the same time more efficient, my mother soon gained the respect and even the affection of the staff. She introduced tea breaks and, perhaps because music had always been so important to her, she installed a radio for them to listen to while they worked. This proved a huge success. Soon they sang along with Bing Crosby's crooning of "White Christmas" or John McCormack's unmistakable voice in "Danny Boy", as well as other popular songs, while the boys whistled in accompaniment. It emerged that Jimmy, the oldest and shyest of them, was very musical and could whistle as beautifully as Bing Crosby himself! As if by magic, the atmosphere in the factory was completely transformed and everyone felt much more at ease. So much so that now, when my parents spoke to one another in German, the girls made a great show of speaking Irish among themselves, though they had not retained much of the language from their compulsory lessons at school. Irish was spoken only in a few remote Gaelic areas across the country but not in Dublin. And so there was much hemming and hawing and, if they did not readily have a word they needed, they invented one. It was clearly meant to be a mild rebuff to my parents, but it was also a certain display of pride, as if to say, "We too have our own language!"

And so began our gradual discovery of Ireland, of the Irish people, their sensitivities, their pride, and above all, their humour.

DUBLIN

Mr. Baron, the headmaster, spoke only English and I could not understand a word of his exchange with my sister, who was enrolling me at the small elementary school I was to attend. But then he suddenly said, "Heil Hitler!" and laughed as he raised his hand in the Nazi salute. The shock I felt must have shown on my face because my sister quickly whispered, "C'est une blague!" (It's a joke) and explained that Mr. Baron had simply said I should say this if I wanted to leave the room. I was very glad that it was my sister who was with me.

The other girls either ignored me or stared at me curiously, while groups of boys followed me on my way home, skipped around me, called out things I could not understand, or poked me with branches until I finally refused to go to school. My sister was then sent to speak to Mr. Baron and explain the situation to him. He promised to put an end to this at once. He would address the entire school at Assembly the very next morning to warn that if he got word of any boy harassing someone during or after school, he would personally administer a good, hard strapping. He kept his promise and after that I was left in peace.

Unfortunately, my father saw no point in higher education for women who, he said, would no doubt marry anyway and stay at home with their children. This meant, sadly, that my sister could not pursue the studies she held so dear and instead worked in my father's factory. For me, life seemed to hold more paradoxes than ever before. My school was a small parochial one, where, except for the Hebrew teacher, the entire staff was Catholic. My father thought I should learn Hebrew as a goodwill gesture toward the small community that had been helpful to him while he was quite alone. However, I stubbornly refused.

Mr. Cassidy, my class teacher, was a lovely man who referred to me as the "foreign girrel." I was fascinated by his pronounced Gaelic accent, as well as by his pale blue eyes and black hair, a combination I had never seen before coming to Ireland. He told me that, since I was still learning English, I should concentrate on that and could do so at the back of the class while every one else was learning Irish, normally a compulsory subject. But Irish was taught by rote, the day's text endlessly repeated by the chorus of voices around me and so eventually, without trying, I too absorbed it and once put up my hand when Mr. Cassidy asked who could recite it and no one else volunteered. After I had done, he held me up as a shining example, "Even the foreign girrel was able to speak Irish," though he must have known full well that I did not understand the meaning of what I was reciting.

My father followed the news closely on the radio as well as in newspapers and when we plied him with questions, did his best to explain, but the political situation was very complicated. In May, 1938 Chamberlain won House of Commons approval for having successfully negotiated an Anglo-Italian Agreement. He spoke warmly of "Italy's new efficiency and vigour under the stimulus of Mussolini's personality" – just as Hitler declared Mussolini to be his "only real friend"! We could see that my father was deeply concerned about this. There were all the usual telltale signs, the way he furrowed his brow, or cupped his hand over pursed lips then suddenly looked up without really seeing anything; the way he shuffled his feet to and fro, to and fro while listening to the radio; and still he defended Chamberlain because, in his view, all Englishmen were honest and honourable.

No sooner had Chamberlain, Mussolini and the French Prime Minister Daladier, met in Munich and agreed not to defend Czechoslovakia, than the Nazi army took possession of it.

"You see?" my mother cried out in anger. "You can't trust anyone! Those poor Czech people! No one reaches out to save them!"

As usual, my father did his best to calm her down, but it was quite clear that he was just as worried as she was, especially when Hitler revealed that he had 462,000 men working on fortifications in the Rhineland, thirty miles deep. How could Chamberlain fly home from Germany after that and promise "Peace for our time"? And what was one to make of the non-aggression pact Germany and Russia signed, with Stalin proposing a toast, "I know how much the German people love their Fuehrer. I should therefore like to drink to his health!"

My father could only shake his head in despair as he tried to unravel all these political machinations for us.

The kaleidoscope of nightmarish headlines was impossible to grasp, much less to digest. One proclaimed that the latest discovery, nuclear fission, could be used to produce weapons of unprecedented power. Another screamed that the IRA had exploded bombs in London, Manchester, Birmingham and other cities. A photo showed Londoners receiving their free air raid shelters. To shelter from whom? It was total confusion.

When, in May of 1939, Stalin proposed a military alliance between Britain, France and Russia, my father doubted this was a genuine offer of goodwill. His doubts were confirmed four months later when, in September, Germany and Russia together invaded Poland. This shook my mother to the core. How could any Russian possibly be on Hitler's side? But then, once Poland was taken and divided between them, Stalin fortunately ceased to cooperate with Germany, because it was at this point that Chamberlain – who had pledged to defend Poland against Hitler – made his announcement in Parliament: "This country is now at war with Germany. We are ready." The die was cast and my father's belief in the honour of Englishmen was vindicated.

Soon war raged over ever-expanding areas. When advances or retreats were announced for either the Allied Forces or the Axis, my father got up, went round his chair to the map he had pinned to the wall and moved small coloured flags to their new positions. Allied advances were devastatingly rare and of short duration. Gradually, city after city across Europe fell to the advancing Germans and the linoleum floor covering under my father's nervously shuffling feet looked more and more scratched and worn.

First Norway and Denmark were taken; then Holland and Belgium fell to the blitzkrieg. When even the French surrendered and Paris was taken, it felt as if the world had come to an end. Paris! We could not believe our ears. Surely this was impossible? Surely it would not be accepted by anyone? It must be a terrible mistake. But the papers showed photos of German troops parading up the Champs Elysées! The Nazi swastika flew from our Arc de Triomphe and at the top of our Eiffel Tower! What of our aunts, uncles and cousins? Would we ever see them again? Would they all be killed? And our friends at the Hôtel de Bretagne – had any of them obtained their visas in time? We had lost touch with all of them.

The small pastel of a young girl lying in a green field, that Francis had painted for me as a parting gift when we left Paris, hung over my bed. I stared at it harder than ever. The tiny pink snout of the little mouse beside her, matched the pink of her barely exposed nipples as she lay back in a peaceful green field. It now felt more precious than ever before. Was any green field in France still untainted with blood?

In neutral Ireland, the German and Japanese Embassies remained open. Were they really the hotbeds of espionage that some claimed? We had no idea what to believe, but despaired at the Irish government's reluctance to support the Allies, and at the general lack of sympathy for their cause that we felt around us. We were shocked to see people wearing swastika rings and lapel pins on the street, on buses and elsewhere. It came as a great relief to hear, some time later, that in spite of this, many Irish people were joining the British forces and a large number were leaving Ireland to work in British factories.

But many others still expressed a wish to see the British beaten, "to teach them" for the hundreds of years of oppression that Ireland had suffered at Britain's hands. We were not familiar with this chapter of Irish history and were unable to relate to it. Was not all of that in the long distant past? The burning issue now was Nazi aggression. It had to be stopped!

But even as I heard my parents and others express such views, and was myself swept up in the underlying emotion and fear, they were still abstractions. The reality of war, the deliberate killing of human beings, was unimaginable – until something or someone close was touched by it – for instance, when the girl who sat next to me in class told me that her older sister's fiancé was fighting on the Eastern front and had not been heard from for a very long time. Neither of us voiced the obvious question. There was no need.

AUNTIE MOLL

In Southern Ireland, life somehow went on. My parents and sister worked at the factory, and I went to school. The rooms we rented were in Auntie Moll's house. Of course, she was not my aunt at all, but it was what everyone called her, and so we did too. She let us have two rooms upstairs, one small one downstairs, and use of the kitchen and bathroom. We could not have lived as cheaply anywhere else. This put us under an obligation to Auntie Moll, which my mother resented. All her life she wanted to be the one to give and found it very hard to be at the receiving end. Besides, my mother strongly disapproved of Auntie Moll, of her heavy makeup, of the company she kept, and most of all of her possible influence on my sister and me.

The first time Mr. William Connor rapped the brass knocker on the front door of that house, my mother went to answer it, then called me because she could not understand what he was saying. If she had not thought that he looked like a gentleman, she certainly would not have bothered.

The hat he deferentially rested against his chest, his sober blue tie, perhaps even his corpulence, and certainly his unwavering gaze as he spoke, combined to impress her. She laid great store by whether or not people looked her straight in the eye.

Mr. Connor wanted to help us think about the future, he said, and I translated for my mother, because, he went on, the future was a chancy thing and we could never count on it, could we? He smiled ingratiatingly. He could not have spoken a truer word. It was a year since we had come to Ireland, forced to leave behind us the future we had worked toward and dreamed of.

Even when it turned out that Mr. Connor was an insurance salesman, his winning charm and very apt words could not be brushed off lightly. My mother asked, and I translated into English, could he come back in the evening when my father would be at home? Then, laughingly, added that the future was something she left to God and her husband. I translated and Mr. Connor beamed. Of course, of course, he would be very happy to come back. And then he said to me, while still looking at my mother, "Tell your mother she's a grand lady." He bowed, donned his hat and was off.

My mother closed the door and went straight to the upstairs window from where she could watch Mr. Connor disappear down the street. "He really is quite a gentleman," she said, more to herself than to me. And then, as an afterthought, "I'm glad he only saw the front of the house. Imagine what he'd think of us if he'd seen the back!"

Our back yard, and all the others close by, were like dumps. Each had an outhouse and a coal shed, and they all overflowed with scrap metal and other rubbish. The butcher's yard was at right angles to ours. He had a shed at one end where he smoked sausages. There was also a biting smell of cat urine, of rotting matter, and over it all hung the rank smell of unrelieved dampness.

Mr. Connor came back the very same evening and my father took him into our small downstairs room. They sat closeted in there for quite some time. My father's low voice was only a hum behind the door, but Mr. Connor's voice rang out quite clearly, especially his laugh.

When the two men at last came out of the room and my father accompanied Mr. Connor back through the hall, my mother joined them and wished him a good evening. He bowed again as he had in the morning and the top of his bald head reflected the hall light. He produced some cigars from his pocket and offered one to my father.

"Real Havanas!" he said, in a stage whisper. "Can't get them for love or money, you know. There's a chappy keeps some for me under the counter."

My father managed one of his rare smiles as he said, "No, thank you. I don't ..."

"What about the lady, then? Not cigars, of course!" Mr. Connor laughed and produced a packet of Gold Flake cigarettes. They were rationed and hard to get, but he insisted that my mother keep the whole lot. She suddenly seemed shy and looked at my father, who translated Mr. Connor's hearty, "It's to celebrate doing business together!" After this my mother did accept his gift. He then took his leave, promising to come back in a few days with the contract.

The next time he came, it was Auntie Moll who opened the door for him. Her peroxide perm shone under the hall light. They had obviously never met before, but immediately got along like a house on fire, and would probably have gone on and on chatting together, if Mr. Connor hadn't caught sight of my father hovering at the back of the hall, waiting for him.

"I might get some insurance too," Auntie Moll said, beaming. "Come in and see me when you're finished."

"The divil wouldn't stop me!" Mr. Connor laughed, waving at her as he walked toward my father.

"What did he say?" my mother asked me. But I did not know what his words meant.

When he had finished with my father, Mr. Connor punctiliously knocked on the parlour door, though Auntie Moll, who was sitting inside, had left it ajar. She closed it as soon as he was with her, but we could still hear them talk and laugh. He stayed in there quite a long while. When he finally emerged, he almost bumped into my mother. He was all smiles and apologies, but she now wore her haughtiest expression and stalked off as if mortally offended.

When he came back the following week to see Auntie Moll, my mother made a great show of going to the upstairs room without

answering his greeting. She continued to follow that pattern whenever he came, which he was to do quite often.

Though I disliked the dirt around us, it didn't trouble me as deeply
as it did my mother. To take a bath was not simple in that house. First
we had to light a fire in the kitchen to heat the boiler. But fuel was
soon in very short supply and rations were small. Consequently, like
everyone else, we bought peat and slag when we could get it, though
both were always wet when delivered and produced far more smoke
than heat. Even when the boiler finally got hot we did not have a
proper bath, but just squatted or knelt to wash under the running tap,
for though my mother scrubbed and scrubbed the deeply encrusted
rings on the tub, they stayed there.

The larger of the two upstairs bedrooms was the only place in our
part of the house that was bright and airy. We used it as a family
room, and often carried our plates upstairs to eat there, watching the
street at the same time.

When Mr. Connor came to call on Auntie Moll we could see him
walking up Wicker Street well before we heard him knock on the
front door. "There he is again!" my mother would say disapprovingly.
If he caught sight of us and waved, my mother quickly ducked without returning his greeting.

I ran into him a few times on the street or in the house, and whenever I did he smiled and made some cheery remark. I grew to like
him and, since I hadn't yet made any friends, I often wished I were old
enough to buy some insurance from him myself. The word "insurance" had a nice comforting ring to it, and it cast a special aura over
Mr. Connor who dispensed it. I kept trying to understand what my
mother had against him, especially since she had seemed to like him
at first, but it was beyond me.

Being a great believer in fresh air, my mother opened the sash
windows wide in the mornings and, when it wasn't raining, hung all
our bedding across the window-sills to air it. But this was not the

custom in Ireland, and people passing by looked askance at it, especially at the enormous feather duvets, the likes of which no one here had ever seen before.

My mother used to pass Auntie Moll's bedroom as quickly as possible. She said it was never aired, but I had a secret fondness for it. It was all pink frills, smelled of powders and perfumes, and was full of little china figurines, yellowed fans, costume jewellery and lots of intriguing little boxes, the contents of which were never revealed. Auntie Moll sometimes called me in there, but I only went if my mother was not at home. The pink curtains were always drawn and the many mirrors reflected pink from all sides. Sometimes I tiptoed in there on my own when I was alone in the house. I pulled the door to behind me, stood in the pink semi-darkness and inhaled the stale, perfume-laden air. It made me feel part of some intimacy to which I couldn't put a name.

The front parlour downstairs was also Auntie Moll's. That was where she entertained her guests and had poker parties. I only saw it from the open door and never went inside. There was a curved "chaise longue" in front of the fireplace – it was the handsomest piece of furniture I had ever seen. When Auntie Moll's friends came to visit, we heard their guffawing all over the house. Sometimes, when they ran out of snacks or cigarettes, she emerged from the smoke-filled room, a cigarette dangling from the corner of her mouth, and asked me to run to the corner store and fetch some more.

If my mother's disapproving face came into view, Auntie Moll would say, "She's just fetching something for me, lovey!"

My mother said nothing, simply drew her lips into her mouth and flashed anger with her eyes, as a lighthouse flashes its beam. Auntie Moll, pretending not to notice – though it would have been impossible not to – pressed money into my hand and went back into her parlour. Only after the door had closed again behind her, did my mother speak her mind.

My father shushed her. "Be careful! Not so loud! You'll offend her, and we'll never find such cheap lodgings again."

My mother then exploded with, "And what about the child? What is it doing to her?"

My father continued to plead for restraint and I escaped, clutching the money tightly in my hand.

When I delivered what I had bought at the parlour door, Auntie Moll urged me to keep the change. I dared not for fear of increasing my mother's wrath, but she kept urging, "Ah, go on, lovey, keep it!" From the doorway I caught sight of the ornate mirror over the mantelpiece, whose reflection doubled the amount of smoke in the room and the number of poker players.

Sometimes we heard them suddenly burst into song in the parlour, popular songs from some film, or an old stand-by, such as "When Irish eyes are smiling," and then Auntie Moll would come out, all smiles and still singing, to fetch the sandwiches she had prepared. Only when she sang did she remove the cigarette that invariably hung from her lips.

No one could put as much feeling into one word as my mother when she said "Poker!", her "p" a small explosion. And when she added "For money!", it felt as if not only gambling, but money itself were the filthiest thing in the world.

Mr. Connor sometimes came to the poker parties now and stayed behind after the others left. I could smell his cigar even before I saw him pass to go to the upstairs lavatory, his shirtsleeves rolled up and the tie around his neck loosened. When my mother heard him come up the stairs humming tunelessly, she quickly pulled me back into the room and said "Filthy!" making a face, as though the very sight of him would soil me for life.

Auntie Moll no longer called him Mr. Connor. He was "Willie" now. She was at her most girlish when Willie was around, and would call up the stairs after him, "Will I make another sandwich, Willie?"

and then, realising what she'd said, she sang out in full voice, "Will I, Willie, will I?" and giggled.

Sometimes Willie wandered into the kitchen before my mother could escape, and she had plenty to say after that – mostly to my father. In front of me, she limited herself to a few terse remarks.

"Disgusting!" or "At their age!" or "In the *front* parlour on a *chaise longue!*"

From then on, whenever the door to the parlour stood open, I gazed at the chaise longue with new interest trying to imagine them on it together.

It never occurred to my mother that she was teaching me the facts of life with her comments and that I might not have noticed anything without her help.

In the mornings I lingered over breakfast while Auntie Moll made her own. I watched her more attentively than ever before. Her aluminium teapot was coated with layers of tannin, and the strong tea came out dark as mud. Her pudgy hand tipped by scarlet nails dug into her Corn Flakes box like a gigantic insect and brought out fistfuls of the cereal, which she put into a bowl. In an unwashed saucepan, thickly coated with layers of yellowed milk deposit, she scalded milk to pour over her Corn Flakes.

"There isn't a bit of use washing it. The milk just sticks on again!" she offered, perhaps in answer to a pointed look from my mother, who worked at her saucepans with steel wool until they shone like mirrors inside and out.

My mother was a small woman, with a knack for speaking volumes without saying a word. Auntie Moll, though a good head taller and much broader, was undoubtedly made to feel uncomfortable in her own home. The more critical my mother was of her, the more I sympathized with her.

It was Auntie Moll who gave me my first cigarette. There was a closed-in space under the stairs with a door and, though my mother was a smoker too, I waited until I was alone in the house to lock myself in there and smoke. My accepting the cigarette and smoking it established a tacit complicity between Auntie Moll and me. We never said much to one another, even when no one else was about. Our worlds remained clearly separate. But every so often our eyes met, and that was enough. It put me in mind of monks in monasteries or nuns in convents who had taken the vow of silence. Of course, we *could* have talked had we chosen to, but we had nothing to say to one another. And so I liked to imagine that we were nuns under the watchful eye of Mother Superior.

I wondered then whether real nuns, too, shared secrets they were not supposed to have. I had never seen so many nuns and priests before coming to Ireland, and was keenly aware of their presence. I looked at them closely when they passed on the street in twos or threes. The ovals of their faces were glowing pink hearts framed by their austere black outfits. Their capacious habits seemed natural places in which to hide things. Under those forbidding black folds, nuns were only human, after all.

I had overheard the girls at my father's factory say it was better to have a sin or two to confess to, rather than arrive empty-handed at confession. They had discussed how awkward it was to have done nothing worth confessing all week, for then what could they tell the priest on Saturday night? It worried them. I gathered that one could not be cleansed if there was nothing to be cleansed of. And what about the poor priest? To be sure, that would put him out of work entirely. And so it was in everybody's interest to have a few sins up one's sleeve.

Auntie Moll used to let me have her magazines when she had finished with them. They were full of love stories with scenes as far removed from our reality as the films we went to see. Of course, films shut out the real world more effectively. In the darkness of the cinema, it was easy to make believe and completely forget our own lives. And it was always a shock to come back out into dimly lit streets where trams rattled, where garbage lay in the gutters and the smell of stale fat from fish and chip shops filled the air. Worst of all was suddenly to catch sight of one's own reflection in a shop window, while standing in a queue at the bus stop, so dreadfully ordinary, so impossibly far removed from those wonderful visions glimpsed on the screen.

However, when reading magazine stories, I could imagine people I knew caught in the situations described, and I cast Auntie Moll and Willie as lovers in some impossible triangle. For fear of being caught reading these romances, I used to hold them inside my open school atlas. They were just about the same size and it worked well.

I would have liked to know, did nuns and priests do the same? Did they, too, sometimes hide things to read inside their prayer books? I wondered, did I share Auntie Moll's sin when I talked to Willie in the hall or in the kitchen and accepted the chocolate bars he brought me? Or when I stood in the semi-darkness of Auntie Moll's pink bedroom? And would her sin have been greater had she brought Willie in there, instead of staying downstairs on the chaise-longue with him? I would have liked to know how sins were graded.

Willie and I became friends. He listened to my halting English with great patience. I liked his hearty laugh and the stories he told.

"Did you hear the one about Yugoslavia?" he asked.

"No," I said.

"*You go slave your* hands off! See? *You go slave your* hands off! Isn't that a good one?"

Another time he asked, "D'you know who invented high heels?"

I shook my head.

"The girl who was kissed on her forehead! Get that? The girl who was kissed on her *forehead*! Ah, sure, we'll soon have you talking like an Irish girl!"

I felt comfortable with Willie. Perhaps I also liked him because he seemed to like me.

I must have been twelve when Auntie Moll slipped me the first daring novel I had ever come across, with the whispered warning, "Mind you don't tell your Mammy, now!" It was about a girl who went out secretly at night to meet her lover, then returned with the bottom of her dress undone. What sort of dress would that be? Perhaps it was a button-down dress. The idea made a very deep impression on me and I felt hot all over every time I re-read that passage. I carried the book from hiding place to hiding place, sure that it wasn't completely safe anywhere. Sometimes I put it under my mattress and then I felt its presence there with my whole body. One night I dreamt that a black man kissed my cheek. When I woke up my cheek still burned. After that, even at school, in the middle of a class, I would suddenly feel those lips on my cheek. The spot that had been kissed would burn and I would close my eyes as a strange new sensation invaded me.

I wondered whether nuns too had books under their mattresses and were they ever left alone long enough to enjoy them? Did they too have dreams about dark men, and would that be considered a sin or not? Since one could not dream on purpose, could dreaming be a sin?

Sin as a concept was uppermost in my mind, but I also thought a great deal about the purely practical aspect of Auntie Moll's moral lapses – for instance, her large pink knickers. Every so often she would wash them and hang them up to dry on a frame held by a pulley attached to the kitchen ceiling, which was where we had to dry all our clothes when it was wet outside. Two large pairs of pink knickers hanging from the ceiling certainly brought that old dark green kitchen to life. To my mother, they were signal flags and she would announce with conviction, "Willie's coming again!"

Naturally I then wondered why, if Willie was filthy, Auntie Moll bothered to wash her knickers before he came and not after.

Willie continued to come to the house intermittently, but with increasingly long absences. During these periods Auntie Moll's swinging step slowed down. She neglected to bleach her hair as soon as new growth appeared and it looked like dusty grass at the edge of the road. Her eyes were no longer the focal point in her face and her painted mouth was like a wound. Friends hardly ever came to see her and sometimes, from the street, I caught sight of her dejectedly looking out of her parlour window.

On a wet December night, shortly before Christmas, I sat alone in the kitchen staring into the fire when Willie's familiar rap sounded on the front door. My parents were still out and Auntie Moll, who was keeping late hours in her menswear shop, had not yet come home. I was lonely and bored and very glad to see Willie's cheerful face. He asked could he come in out of the rain and wait. I just smiled and stood aside to let him in, thinking how happy Auntie Moll would be when she came home and found him there.

He went straight into the parlour but a few minutes later, stood in the kitchen doorway, saying, "I'll just warm myself here at the fire for a minute." I was glad of his company, but wondered why he did not warm himself at the electric fire in the front room.

"Will I make you a cup of tea?" I echoed Auntie Moll, sure she would be pleased at my making Willie feel at home.

"That'd be grand!" he said and watched me cross the kitchen to the sink in the scullery to fill the kettle. Suddenly I felt nervous with Willie's eyes following me so closely. The matches were damp and, under his watchful gaze, I fumbled with them unable to light one. Finally one did light, but it broke under my finger.

"Here, let me!" he said, his beefy fingers gripping the box in my hand. I saw that his nails were broken and dirty as he deftly struck a match and lit the gas.

As I put the kettle on, I unexpectedly caught sight of Willie's face in the small mirror that hung on the wall near the stove. It was a cheap thing that distorted all images. Willie's face looked grotesque, his nose flattened and broadened, his lips twisted protrusions. The next instant I smelled his sweat and the stale cigar smoke on his breath as he said into my ear, "Ah, you're a grand girl!" and cupped my breasts in his hands.

For a moment I stood frozen to the ground. The rain was battering the kitchen window, the fire was crackling and the gas hissed under the kettle. All at once I heard Auntie Moll's key in the door.

I ran out of the kitchen and up the stairs into the bathroom, bolting the door. My legs shook so hard I could hardly stand as I cupped cold water in my hands and held it to my throbbing face. When I looked into the mirror, the blemishes and scratches on its surface covered the face that stared back at me.

We continued to live in Auntie Moll's house. But Willie no longer called.

THE WINDOW

When my mother spoke Russian, as she often continued to do to my father, especially if she did not want us to understand, we usually guessed the gist of what she was saying, though we did not know the language. But in the German she had learned while living in that country, in the French she had picked up in France and soon, in the English that she acquired in Ireland, we were well aware that she could call a spade a spade. How I envied her that skill! Mrs. Holländer, a German friend in Dublin, a hefty woman twice my mother's size, once told my mother how carefully she observed her diet but still lost no weight. My mother exclaimed in German, "Von nichts kommt nichts!" (Nothing comes of nothing.) Mrs. Holländer pleaded that she had cut down on bread and never touched cakes. My mother raised her dark eyebrows, "And what about butter? And chicken fat?" At this Mrs. Holländer's face fell as she stammered, "I only use them for cooking." My mother then shrugged, "You see!" Such exchanges often embarrassed me, and I couldn't help feeling a little sorry for Mrs. Holländer. But more than anything, I envied my mother her ability to speak up.

In the evenings after we had eaten, my father sat glued to the radio – head down and, with grave concentration – listening to the BBC News. When, during the course of the news, parts of Hitler's speeches were broadcast, his every pause filled by thousands of people cheering and shouting, "Heil Hitler!", my mother, though she trembled, cried out with true Slav abandon, "Why doesn't someone stuff a boiling potato into his mouth?" (If only someone had listened to her, how it might have altered the course of history!) Suddenly, after she had said this, it no longer seemed as if the end of the world had come! Suddenly this monster who personified evil, was reduced to human proportions: his mouth, like any other mouth, could be scalded! He was vulnerable and so, clearly, not invincible. Such comments often helped me regain some perspective.

When Mrs. Holländer came to visit, she sat with us at the red lacquered coffee table, on one of two matching chairs – the only three pieces of furniture rescued from our old house in Frankfurt. Some-one had taken them and our bulky bedding out of Germany before war broke out, and shipped them to us across the English Channel and the Irish Sea. I never understood why these items were singled out when nothing else was saved. Now, in Dublin, we slept with our old feather duvets and the red set stood at the window of the upstairs bedroom, the one bright spot in our rented rooms. In Germany, the square table had had a glass top under which my mother used to place a small round lace cloth, its whiteness contrasting nicely with the red lacquered wood that showed through. Somewhere en route the glass top had been broken, but the metal clamps that had once held it were still attached to the table edges. Like us, I thought.

This was where my mother sat when she had mending to do, or potatoes to peel or any other task she could take upstairs, away from the dark, drafty kitchen that faced the miserable backyard. At that upstairs window she could watch the neighbours come and go. When I sat across from her, eating my breakfast or doing my homework, there was no need to lift my head, for my mother told me every-thing that happened out there. In the mornings she saw who left for work and at what time; she saw the butcher, his cap pulled down, leave for his shop, and remarked, "He always looks unwashed!" She saw our landlady, Auntie Moll, who occupied half the house, leave for her menswear shop downtown. "Again a new hat!" my mother would comment, and I guessed at once whom she meant by her tone. She had a clear view of who entered the rabbi's house to consult him about this or that, and watched for the callers to leave again and the rabbi to nod them on their way. It was my mother's way of keeping up with the world, at least the part of it where we had now settled.

Once she sent me to the rabbi to show him a chicken she had disemboweled. It had a diseased liver, and the rabbi would know whether or not the rest of the chicken was kosher and could be eaten. Never having encountered a rabbi before and certainly never having spoken to one, I was very nervous. Before coming to Ireland, religion had not been part of our lives. But the rabbi turned out to be a very mild man and pronounced the chicken to be fine. He also said that his much younger sister, Sarah, who was in my class at school, had told him that I read a lot of books. "Even books about atoms!" he said. (I'd borrowed this book from the library to help me understand a story in a comic about a group of people who made themselves so tiny that they could enter the atoms inside a coin, but the book proved too difficult for me.) His remark immediately worried me: had his sister also told him about my "illegal" copy of Darwin's "On the Origin of Species"? At the time, it was banned in Ireland. What stand would a rabbi take in a Catholic country where to read this book was a sacrilegious act and merely possessing it was breaking the law? But to my great relief the rabbi's sister had not betrayed me, for he patted me on the shoulder and said, "It's very good to read!" Sarah and another friend who was Catholic, separately tried to save my soul. In a way their concern pleased me – no friend in France had ever worried about me quite like this.

It was at the same red table that my mother received Professor L., a passionate linguist. He came to speak Russian to my mother. She was grateful, for – apart from her one-sided exchanges with my father, who answered in German – she knew no one else in Dublin with whom she could speak her native tongue. She had lost all contact with her family in the Soviet Union since we had left France. Having learnt to be extremely cautious in the uncertain political climate of the time, she dared not make any enquiries about their whereabouts or their welfare. It might have attracted attention and thus spelled possible danger for her family – or for us. Tragically, she was never able to find trace of them again.

Perhaps because Professor L. saw how painfully shy I was, he encouraged me to visit his home. And so I sometimes cycled along the walled roads that wind around and up into the Dublin Mountains, to the old rambling house where he lived with his wife, a son and also a daughter who was a single parent with a little boy of about eighteen months.

Convinced that language is innate and not learned, Professor L. saw his grandson's birth as a golden opportunity to prove a pet theory. The child's father was Vietnamese. The little boy had a sweet face and gentle disposition but no one was allowed to utter a word in his presence. Professor L's experiment consisted of waiting for the child to produce sounds, or primitive words not learned from others, but which would be his very own, inherited from his Vietnamese forbears.

No one was unkind to the little boy. They played with him, and took him for walks in the surrounding countryside, but they never spoke in his presence. He was put into a playpen out of earshot before the family sat down and talked. It seemed strange and cruel to me that both his mother and grandmother complied fully with the grandfather's dictates and saw nothing wrong with enforcing the required isolation and silence. But then, to my shame, I did not stand up for him either, although I desperately wanted to.

My mother wouldn't have hesitated to do so. She was marvelous at pricking the bubble of other people's illusions. Had she visited that family with me, one pointed remark from her might have shown how ludicrous the grandfather's idea was. Besides, she could not bear to see cruelty of any kind, particularly if directed at some helpless victim, human or animal.

Years later, I saw the boy again. He seemed no different from others his age. Still, I feel guilty to this day for having been a silent witness to what might well have been very damaging to a young child.

When a neighbour, Mr. Klein, fell ill my mother only had to lean forward very slightly on her red chair at the window to see Dr. Robinson, who was our doctor too, return again and again to the Kleins' house. He came without delay whenever he was called, carrying the black bag that he never opened because, without instruments or tests, he was able to diagnose all ills with incredible accuracy. A short man with a large head and the kindest face I had ever seen, he had once hoped to become a concert violinist. His name was still in the orchestra pit of the Gaiety Theatre where he had engraved it while playing there. Some years later my mother consulted him about her heart trouble. After that, whenever he saw her, he smiled and, in his gentle voice, asked, "And how is the old ticker today?"

When air-raid sirens shrieked while German bombers flew over Dublin – by mistake they claimed – and their bombs plummeted through the soft Irish mist with a terrifying whistle, my mother ran to the same window, her hands hugging her belly, pregnant with my younger sister, then rocked to and fro while invoking the mercy of a God in whom she did not quite believe.

And when Mr. Klein died, my mother sat at that window and shivered, watching people arrive for the funeral; she rocked to and fro, biting her handkerchief to cope with the pain; and she shook with sobs when the coffin was carried out of the house, although she had hardly known Mr. Klein. But she was crying for Mr. Klein's wife; for the four children who had lost their father; for the time Mr. Klein had greeted her in such a friendly way; she cried for her own parents whom she had never seen again after she married a foreigner and left her native Russia with him, and for not knowing when or how they had died and who had carried their coffins; she cried for the baby son, my little brother, who had died at six months and whose coffin she had not been allowed to see because she was so broken after his death; she rocked and sobbed and wailed for the sorrow that coffins everywhere signal.

THE CLOSING OF A CHAPTER

When three nephews of Auntie Moll's suddenly came to Dublin, two from England and one from Scotland, we guessed at once that they had come to evade conscription. What cowards! I thought, condemning all three out of hand. By this time the war was no longer confined to places we could find on my father's map of Europe. Allied troops were engaged on many different fronts across the world. After Pearl Harbour, when the Americans joined in, it all became even harder to follow.

In oceans everywhere, ships were being sunk indiscriminately. Bombs, then rockets were targeting the most vulnerable areas. It became quite impossible to think of all these events as part of one single war between the forces of good and evil. Instead it was a nightmarish blur of bloodshed and atrocities.

I came to like the Scottish nephew, Julian, and began to defend him in my own mind: he was right not to want to kill. It simply proved how sensitive he was. I now thought him wise and looked up to him. I decided there had to be other ways of stopping aggressors. It was obvious that most men must like the idea of going to war to prove how brave and strong they were, otherwise wars would not have been fought throughout history! Viewed logically, from my perspective – I was thirteen now – the solution was simple: to persuade all men to refuse to fight; then even a dictator would be rendered powerless! I never voiced these thoughts to anyone, least of all to Julian in whose presence I was even more tongue-tied than usual. But I did feel they were important and wrote them down into what became lengthy diatribes.

The only person to whom I showed my writing was Brenda, a girl three years older than I, who had befriended me. She was a Quaker and told me that many Quakers were conscientious objectors and refused to go on active service. When they were called up, they only agreed to tend the wounded or participate in some other passive role. She also told me about the Quaker Peace Testimony, a summons to action rather than a belief, that calls on Quakers to oppose war and seek other means to settle disputes between people and countries. Brenda took me along to meetings at the Friends' House on Eustace St., and it seemed wonderful to me that no one officiated here. Instead, any member of the congregation could stand up and speak his mind. This discovery and Brenda's encouragement bolstered my confidence enough for me to share my feelings with her, if not with others. But I never mentioned Julian to her or to anyone else, too conscious of the inadequacy of my defense. I wished he would show some interest in settling international disputes or in driving an ambulance, but continued to tell myself that he must have his reasons for staying in Dublin.

Auntie Moll always seemed delighted when her nephews came to see her. When Julian was with them, I found excuses to stay nearby. He treated me with respect, almost as if I were grownup, whereas his two cousins appeared not even to see me. But then it dawned on me that they came mostly to see my sister, and that this was true of Julian, too. She was intelligent, quick-witted and of course the right age, not just a young teenager like me. They got along very well and she clearly enjoyed their company, most of all Julian's. I could see why. He was special, quite unlike anyone else we knew. He spoke of many things philosophically, expressing himself eloquently in his low-key, charming lilt and often spoke to her as if no one else were present. It was no surprise that she enjoyed his attention. Or that he should single her out. But when he asked her to go for long walks with him and she accepted, it put a different complexion on everything in my eyes and upset me deeply. I then reverted to my original judgment of him and of his cousins. All three of them had run away from the war! They were cowards, shirking their duty! Allowing others to get killed in their place! How could they? And how could my sister accept and condone this?

The war dragged on and spread. Britain reported an acute man-power shortage in the Forces as well as in factories. Women of up to forty years old – both single and married – were being conscripted. Even boys and girls between sixteen and eighteen now had to register. The brutal conflict seemed never-ending ... and in two years I would be sixteen! Since I spoke German, could I not be trained as a spy? "Was für ein Unsinn!" ("What madness!") said my father.

We were sheltered from the war but lived it vicariously. All the while, our day-to-day lives continued as normally as circumstances permitted. My mother gave birth to my younger sister, Vivienne. For me she was a live doll whom I loved deeply. I wanted to be her second mother. My older sister met someone new and soon got married. This did not cause any estrangement between us, on the contrary. She did not move far away, and we now spent more time together than before. It felt very special to visit her in the loft apartment where she and her husband lived. We gradually grew closer with a new understanding. After she had moved out and I took over her room, I found an undated letter to her from Julian which, to my shame, I read. He wrote as he spoke, philosophically, even in the way he told her that he had tuberculosis. I was overcome with guilt for having judged him.

American and Canadian soldiers, stationed in the British North, spent their days on leave in Dublin, and could be seen everywhere. They came partly to eat steaks and eggs to their hearts' content. In Britain neither could be had, whereas our rationing only applied to anything imported.

But Britain soon sealed off Ireland, in a bid to prevent details of Allied invasion preparations from reaching Dublin, and then to be relayed to Berlin by spies. This dramatic move was made after President de Valera refused to expel enemy diplomatic and consular envoys, as President Roosevelt requested. The Irish President held that such action would breach Ireland's neutrality.

The day dawned at last when the Allies began to gain ground in Africa, in Burma, in the Philippines, and gradually, also in Europe. It was hard to believe that the tide was really turning and that all this would one day stop. But headlines did claim that the Germans were on the run throughout Europe, even on the Russian front, and the Allied leaders were confident. There were already plans afoot to create a new worldwide organization for preserving peace. It would be called the United Nations and all peace-loving nations would be invited to join. "No would-be aggressor should ever get started", said President Roosevelt.

Yet battles, killings and reprisals continued for another seemingly endless year, before we heard the news which hundreds of thousands of people were hoping and praying for. When it finally came, on 30th April, 1945, "The Fuehrer has killed himself!", no one could at first take it in.

Two days later, we were shocked to learn that the Irish President and Joseph Walshe, Secretary of the Dept. of External Affairs, had called at the home of Eduard Hempel, German Minister to Ireland, to express their condolences on the death of Adolf Hitler. It did, at least, confirm that he really was dead, but a full sense of deliverance only came a few days later, on May 7th, when Churchill announced the unconditional surrender of Nazi Germany and the end of Hitler's Third Reich.

In Europe the nightmare had ended. All fighting had stopped. But in Japan the worst was yet to happen, in Hiroshima and Nagasaki, before an unequivocal surrender in August of that year.

Still, on that May day, the relief was indescribable! Everyone was jubilant, even those who had, at best, been "neutral". The atmosphere was wonderfully festive, laden with laughter and good cheer and talk and hugging, even among total strangers. Everyone shared in the sense of elation and giddiness. No one had ever felt so free and light-hearted!

My sister, her husband, two friends and I went out for dinner – an unheard of luxury for me. They chose "The Unicorn", a restaurant on Merrion Row, run by a Viennese friend. The meal was the jolliest I had ever had. We drank wine and raised our glasses in endless toasts to everything and everyone. Afterwards, all of us slightly tipsy, we walked along Stephen's Green then down Grafton Street, singing at the top of our voices. On another occasion, a man was arrested on this same street for walking the length of it in his pyjamas in broad daylight – for a bet. Had he done so on this day instead, no one would have stopped him.

Everyone felt liberated and tolerant of everyone else.

We sang all the national anthems we knew, including Russia's "Internationale", since Russia, too, had fought hard on the Allied side. Not that we knew the words, but any old words were just fine. The crowds around us sang their own songs or shouted. On approaching the entrance to Trinity College, we saw a number of students on the roof over the main entrance. They were waving Union Jacks and singing "God Save the Queen" and "Rule Britannia". Then other students hoisted a Red Flag, a French Tricolor and at the very bottom of the mast, an Irish tricolour. This was followed by a scuffle of some kind and someone set fire to the Irish flag. A large crowd immediately gathered around the gates and we left as quickly as we could.

No matter, it had been the best day of my life!

By this time, Ireland, its culture and the spirit of its people, had seeped into our blood and become an integral part of us, although no Irish person would have recognized this. We were not aware of it ourselves until long after we had left that country.

POSTWAR TRAVEL

At the war's end, we were impatient to hear from family members and were terribly excited when their first telegrams and letters arrived. As soon as there were flights to Belgium, my father decided to fly there to see his youngest sister, Selma, and her husband Arthur, the aunt and uncle who had been first to leave Germany and had taken me with them. We had not seen them since that time.

My mother accompanied my father to the airport to see him off – both were equally nervous about this new airborne mode of travel and sat close together in the departure lounge, waiting for the fateful announcement of my father's flight. After a while they were told that the thick fog shrouding Dublin made a take-off impossible and the flight had to be postponed. Somewhat relieved at this reprieve, they returned home to find a telegram from Brussels, saying "Leo arrived safely. Has already eaten carp." My uncle Arthur had had this ready to send the moment my father arrived; then, on hearing there would be a delay but not knowing its cause, sent the telegram anyway to reassure my mother who, he thought, would be all the more anxious. Carp was my father's favourite fish and could not be had in Ireland. We all had a good laugh and that broke my parents' tension. His flight was rescheduled and all ended well.

Quite early during the German occupation of Belgium, uncle Arthur and his younger brother were arrested by the Gestapo, then sent to an internment camp in the North of France. By some miracle they both managed to escape after two years, and later learned that none of the other internees of that camp had survived. Making their way back to Belgium on foot was a long and arduous trek, especially since they had to hide during the day and only walked after dark. They reached Brussels after many narrow escapes and somehow found my aunt, whom a very brave and kind neighbour was hiding in a cellar. Now all three of them hid in that cellar until the war ended and, like so many others in hiding across Europe, they spent much of their time listening to the BBC's "Radio Free Europe" broadcasts and the "Voice of America". Their daughter, a younger cousin I was yet to meet, was safely hidden in a convent. To our astonishment, even Astor, their dog, had survived.

The end of the war brought a sense of euphoria, but despite all his bravery and sense of humour, my uncle never really recovered from what he had been through. The full extent of the damage he suffered I only learned a few months later, when I accepted their invitation to spend a year with them in Brussels.

My first flight out of Ireland in early 1946, was to France to see those of our relatives who had survived in that country. All were deeply affected by the trauma of the war years – an aunt, an uncle, friends. I was filled with guilt at their pitiful state, guilt at my immediate family's luck, safely sheltered in neutral Ireland, while they lived through the hell of pursuit and constant fear of discovery that marked them forever. One aunt, Ivo, not well enough to return to Paris, had stayed in Luchon, in the South of France, where she had been hidden by local people. I went to see her first, taking a small aircraft from Paris that was barely fit for passengers. On the Aer Lingus flight from Dublin, the stewardess had handed each passenger a printed prayer asking God to keep the aircraft safe. I almost wished there were such prayers on this French flight. Commercial travel, in its infancy before the war, was then only slowly resuming. This small plane had no proper seats, only a couple of benches along its sides and glaring bullet holes in several places, and it hopped along at low altitude through air pockets in a far from reassuring way.

The visit with my aunt Ivo was very sad. My mother and she had been very close in Paris. She had taken a course in dressmaking when my mother took hers in millinery and then spent her days in my mother's little hotel room, working alongside her, sometimes making a dress for me out of leftover fabric. Although she recognized me now, she was not even capable of having a proper conversation with me. I stayed with her for a few days, and when I took my leave, wondered whether she would remember my visit afterwards.

In Paris my father's middle brother, Herman, his wife Leska, a cousin, Ruth, and I shared many bittersweet moments, happiness at seeing one another and deep sadness about those who had perished. Ruth, to whom I had been closest when we were little, was the child of my father's youngest brother, Feddie (Ferdinand). She was saved by a Parisian family. They had her renamed Françoise and successfully concealed her real identity, but tragically, her parents were deported and died in Auschwitz.

Uncle Herman, with whom I was staying, had fled to North Africa and volunteered for the French Foreign Legion. Miraculously, he lived through incredible experiences as a légionnaire in active service. His motto after that, he said jokingly, was "Never join anything voluntarily!" When the war ended, he managed to return to his wife, who had stayed in hiding in southern France. Another cousin, Lucien, had joined the Résistance and was never heard of again.

Looking at Françoise and listening to her, no one could have guessed at her frustration, or the effort it had cost her to learn French as a little girl. I clearly remembered her sitting on the floor, her arms around her knees, as she tearfully repeated the names of the days of the week over and over, trying to get the order and the pronunciation right and never quite making it. Now she was completely French in every way and married to the son whose parents had saved her life.

She had not yet wholly absorbed the shock of her own parents' horrific fate – the Red Cross had only recently notified her of their findings. The full realization of what had happened came to her gradually, over time, after she received a package containing the physical evidence of a few scraps of their clothing that were recovered in Auschwitz.

For the present, she clung to her immediate life. It was important for us to be together, even if briefly, to be able to recall happy moments shared in France, when the whole family had still been there; when my sister had written plays in verse for us to perform for the adults – in German of course, for that was the language they continued to speak among themselves. We could still recall some of my sister's carefully rhyming lines that we had learned by heart,

Ich hab' gegessen und getrunken
Und auch ein bisschen Schlaff gefunden …

(I have eaten and drunk and also found a little sleep …)
and we laughed with tears in our eyes.

Françoise had met me at the airport, helped me retrieve the luggage I had left there in safekeeping while I traveled further, and brought me to Uncle Herman's apartment. Both he and my aunt were at work. I was about to begin unpacking, to give her some of the gifts I had brought, but she urged me to leave all that for later. First, she would take me around Paris, to see familiar places.

Unlike London where large areas had been reduced to rubble, Paris had not suffered any bomb damage, deliberately spared by the Germans because it was coveted by Hitler as his "prize". But no matter where we went, I was conscious of an all-enveloping shroud of wretchedness. Everything was a dull grey and visibly neglected. Outwardly at least, the city was intact, but showed no sign of the old buoyancy, the joie de vivre that I remembered. No one had yet recovered from the bitterness of defeat or the humiliation of the Nazi occupation. Personal animosities lingered, accusations of collaboration with Germans festered, but there was also widespread open hatred. Françoise told me not to believe the frequent claims I would hear from people of how they personally had opposed the enemy. In truth, only a small percentage of the population had done so.

On the bus, I opened my handbag and Françoise, catching sight of my passport, warned me not to carry it around with me. There were too many pickpockets everywhere, she said, and next time I should leave it in the apartment. I said that I would. But to our horror, on our return we found the front door standing open, the apartment burgled and many things missing, including my unopened suitcases. The latter were probably what had attracted the burglars' attention. They must have seen us arrive with bulging luggage, then leave the apartment without it. We felt devastated on my uncle's and aunt's behalf. To have their very few possessions stolen at this point, after all they had lived through, was a particularly cruel blow.

Uncle Herman had always been the bon-vivant, the optimist in the family, insisting on good times, especially as an antidote, when it was the last thing on anyone's mind. On the following day he said it was unthinkable for me to visit Paris without having a taste of its nightlife, and promptly bought a ticket for me to the Casino de Paris. To go alone? I was horrified, protesting that I had never been to "such a place", that I wouldn't know what to do or how to behave. I was naïve, only eighteen, had grown up in prudish Ireland and did not feel equal to this. But he refused to listen to my pleas, insisted that it was just like any theatre, that I would simply have to go in and find my seat. He would escort me to the door and pick me up after the performance. I suspect he could not afford more than one ticket, or he and my aunt would surely have come with me.

No one could have felt more nervous or self-conscious than I as, head down, I crept into the theatre and found my seat. At that time, a law forbade any nude person on stage from moving and so the program consisted mainly of static tableaux in which men and women in varying degrees of nudity, posed as provocatively as possible. I sat through it tight-lipped, hands on knees, so tense that they might have been welded together. Shortly before the end, an elegant woman came out on stage. She was clad in a tight-fitting black velvet gown that covered her entirely from chin to ankles. She stood still for a moment then began to rotate very slowly until she had her back turned to the audience, revealing a very large heart-shaped hole in her gown that exposed her "derrière". Everyone burst out laughing and applauded. I did neither, just sat there rigidly. Suddenly, my neighbour, a man with an unmistakably British moustache, bent toward me and asked, "I say, are you English?"

STAYS ABROAD

Later that year, I accepted an invitation from Selma and Arthur to spend a year with them in Brussels. This gave us the opportunity to reconnect properly and for me to become acquainted with my cousin, some years younger than I. We shared many warm, intimate moments recalling, among much else, how Arthur used to put an opera recording on his record-player as soon as he heard me clamber up the steps to their apartment in Frankfurt, then make me guess which opera it was. Now, in Brussels, he took us to concerts in the famed Palais des Beaux Arts. It was thrilling for me to hear internationally known soloists perform, none of whom had yet found their way to Dublin. But all was not light-hearted. I soon became aware of how seriously Arthur had been affected by his wartime experiences. His condition was far from stable and he had to undergo extremely difficult treatment. Fortunately, Selma was resilient, and able to support and encourage him.

Sadly, other people, some of whom were close friends, had suffered even worse fates. When we visited them, it was impossible to think of anything positive to say. One was simply tongue-tied in face of the nightmare they had lived, too horrendous for them to overcome – ever.

It is almost unbearable, even now, 70 years later, to think about one close friend whom we called Tante Patch. She was the kindest, warmest person imaginable, and hers was surely the worst cross of all to bear. Her husband and two sons had gone into hiding but she was afraid that they would be found, and persuaded them that it would be safer to comply with the Gestapo's dictate, namely that all Jewish men and boys register officially. They followed her advice, were deported at once and she never saw them again.

At least Selma and Arthur had one another and their child.

After my year in Belgium, I had occasion to go to Denmark and found it to be quite a contrast to both France and Belgium. By then, three years had passed since the war's end, but no European country had yet recovered from it. Denmark had not suffered bombardments or other physical damage and, unlike the French and the Belgians, Danes had either retained or reacquired a cheery outlook and a great ability to enjoy life.

In Denmark as elsewhere, there were still many shortages. Nothing was being imported yet, and even homegrown foods were either very scarce or unavailable, as were most commodities. But none of this impeded life.

I remember the thrill a friend, Florence, and I felt on seeing the first record in a Copenhagen music store. We dashed inside and bought it, though this recording of a Mozart horn concerto did not particularly interest either of us. But it proved irresistible. Nothing like it had been available for years. We took it back to the boarding-house and, with great excitement, cranked up the gramophone and played it.

Florence and I both taught English at the Berlitz School of Languages. We were a motley crew of instructors, hailing from many different parts of the world. Florence was Welsh and had a lovely voice and after our late classes, she and I would often walk together along the nighttime *Stróget*, Copenhagen's liveliest street where the Berlitz School was located, and sing Schubert Lieder or whatever else came to mind. Without Florence to urge me on, I would not have had the courage to sing out loud on the street. I once told her that I could never recall the melody of Dvorak's 10th Slavonic Dance, although it was my favourite. She said that since it was such a sad melody, I only needed to let my head hang down, and it would come to me. This worked like magic! From then on, just *thinking* about letting my head hang was enough to bring the melody to mind instantly.

The famed new concert hall, unique at the time, in Copenhagen's *Radiohuset* had recently been completed. Its walls and high ceiling, all clad in beautiful teak wood, were a wonder to behold, and their acoustic effect had an almost palpable glow. We could not afford the price of concert tickets but could attend rehearsals at no charge. And so we heard some very fine performances under the baton of Russian-born Nikolai Malko, whose most celebrated pupil was Shostakovich. He occasionally invited famous virtuosi, such as the legendary Pablo Casals whose grunts, clearly audible above his brilliant cello-playing, are still fresh in my memory. Malko had helped to establish the Danish State Radio Symphony Orchestra and at a later point, the very popular Danish King, Frederick IX, named him Knight of the Order of Dannebrog. To everyone's delight, the Danish Royal family was very close to the people. They could be seen going into or coming out of the Castle, which was right downtown. The King himself often cycled through the streets of Copenhagen and people waved to him; some even called out, "Hello Freddie!"

Compared to poverty-stricken Ireland, Denmark was quite a contrast, although there was no sign of affluence – on the contrary. But buildings and streets, buses and trams, all were well-maintained. Everything seemed to sparkle. I speak here of the late 1940s and early 1950s, and many aspects of life have radically changed in both countries in the intervening years. But at that time, nothing in Denmark remotely resembled what I had seen in Ireland, especially the state of the Irish poor. No one went hungry, there were no beggars on the streets, and illiteracy was practically unknown. I was struck by how well everything functioned, by the efficiency and cleanliness everywhere, by how orderly life was in this model, pragmatic country. It prided itself on the fairness of its democratic political system with reason and, to me, seemed like a Utopia. Its welfare system, trade unions, and social and healthcare programs were far in advance of most, if not all, other western countries.

But oh, I did miss Ireland!

Perhaps I voiced these feelings a little too emphatically to a Danish journalist friend, because he then said to me, accusingly, "You think we have no soul in this country! But we do! The only difference between the Irish and us is that we don't wear ours on our sleeves as they do."

I did not mean to put down Danes. To this day I am in regular touch with wonderful Danish friends to whom I still feel very close. But while I lived in that tidy little country, I longed for the individuality of Irish people, their rebelliousness, inventiveness, quick wit, and, above all, the poetry that permeates the language and is part of the Irish spirit. I missed the shopkeeper whom I asked for a dozen eggs, and who instead of giving them to me, said, "They're very dear today! Wouldn't six do you?"; and the steward on the boat from Holyhead to Dun Laoghaire to whom I apologized for not being able to leave a larger tip, who then looked most concerned and asked, "Are you sure you have enough left for yourself, Miss?"

I missed the shop assistant in the store where I had sent a visiting Canadian friend, to replace a broken leather strap on her bulging suitcase: the assistant asked, "Why don't you just use a piece of rope?" I longed for the inefficiency in Ireland and the haphazard way things got done or not done; for the surprises, for the hundred springs in every Irish winter. In Denmark, even the seasons knew their place. During my years there, I went back to Ireland several times. Both the North Sea and the Irish Sea can be extremely rough in summer and winter, and I am not a good sailor. But it was worth facing their storms to fill a deep need for that other way of looking at the world and coping with it. It somehow provided a sense of equilibrium.

ANOTHER BEGINNING

It did not feel like a new beginning, but more like a continuation, because of the instant sense of recognition I had when I met the man who became my husband. Werner had come to study in Ireland but his history was not unlike mine. His family, too, had fled from Germany in the mid 1930s, but they had gone to South Africa where they had an extremely difficult beginning. To make a living, his parents tried to sell ties, suspenders and other small wares from door to door, just as my father had done when he first arrived in Ireland. But before long, both parents fell seriously ill, and Werner and his younger brother were taken to an orphanage. They stayed there for four years, waiting for their father's health to improve and then for him to scratch together a living in the hardware trade until he could earn enough to support his family.

The boys had not been unhappy at the orphanage. It was run along strict lines, but not in an oppressive way, and the children were treated well. Sometimes on Saturday evenings, a "nice man" who was an amateur astronomer came to give slide shows of the heavens' wonders. Among the planets shown, Jupiter and Saturn with its rings particularly fired Werner's imagination. His father noted this when the family was reunited, although he had little time or energy to spend on his children. And so, when he happened to see a pedlar passing with an old set of *Chambers' Encyclopedia* in his cart, he called to him and, in exchange for an old suit, got the nine volumes that were in the cart – one was missing, luckily not the volume that included astronomy.

When Werner subsequently announced that he wanted to become an astronomer, his father discouraged him. "It's not a good profession," he said, "You have to stay up all night to look at the sky, and the pay is poor!" Werner paid no attention to this warning. Poring over the encyclopedia articles was the beginning of his lifelong fascination, not only with the night sky, but with the universe as a whole.

His father never recovered his health fully and, very sadly, died at the early age of forty-nine. This happened when Werner, then nineteen, was studying for his B.Sc. degree. There was no one else who could replace his father in the store and it fell to Werner to do so. Studying at the same time was almost impossible and, as soon as he obtained his degree, he suspended further studies to devote himself full time to the store.

Four years later, in 1954, a lucky break allowed him to return to University where he quickly obtained a Master's degree and simultaneously won two scholarships to study abroad. What a wrench it must have been for his mother to let him go! But surely it was difficult for him as well, being all too aware of leaving her to fend for herself and for his younger brother. Still, she understood that he was destined for the sciences, and she was supportive even when he decided to go half a world away from where she was.

Of the many places where he might have gone, Werner chose the Dublin Institute for Advanced Studies, and applied to its Director, Erwin Schrödinger, a Nobel laureate, popularly known for his cat paradox. De Valera, who had been a high school mathematics teacher before entering politics and ever a devotee of theoretical physics, was greatly impressed with Schrödinger's achievements, and moved heaven and earth to bring him to Ireland. To this end, he had founded the Dublin Institute for Advanced Studies in 1940 and invited Schrödinger to be the Director of its School of Theoretical Physics. Schrödinger accepted and held the post for the next sixteen years.

But just at the time Werner wrote to him, Schrödinger had decided to return to his native Vienna. He therefore passed Werner's application on to the new Director, J.L. Synge, whom Werner also much admired, and it was he who then invited Werner to come to Dublin. (J.L. Synge happened to be the nephew of the Irish playwright John Millington Synge, a poetic dramatist of great power and co-founder of Dublin's famous Abbey Theatre.)

Werner was familiar with J.L. Synge's research, in particular his construction of the first complete picture of a black hole's interior. Synge had done this ground-breaking work five years earlier, before the study of black holes became fashionable and before they were called by that name. Subsequently, Werner's own interest in black holes became a lifelong exploration.

Werner set sail for England in 1956, and continued on to Ireland. On his arrival in Europe, he rediscovered a world he did not remember, where white women carried their own luggage and white men rode bicycles. How different it felt from the environment he had left behind in South Africa with its apartheid system! Racial separation had always been a fact of life there, from the very beginning of white colonization, but in 1948 it was enacted into law and had grown harsher from then on. Among other rules that were strictly enforced, all native black people were obliged to leave the cities after work and go back to the townships in which they were forced to live.

Only one year earlier, in June of 1955, at the African National Congress in Johannesburg, Nelson Mandela and 156 other leaders were charged with treason. Their "crime" was to have formulated the Freedom Charter setting out their vision of a new South Africa, a united, non-racial and democratic South Africa that would belong to all who lived in it. For seeking to make this vision a reality, Nelson Mandela was banished to Robben Island to serve a twenty-seven-year prison sentence. Such events made up the daily reality of life in South Africa. Europe was a different world.

We met casually at the house of a mutual friend, a charming

elderly Hungarian, Cornelius Lanczos, who was a Senior Professor at the Institute. He had an endless fund of stories to tell that he related to whatever topic was under discussion, thus immediately putting everyone at their ease. This proved to be most helpful, as both Werner and I were shy and socially hesitant. From when we first met, there was never a moment's doubt. We soon married, both of us inveterate dreamers. Before long it became clear that one of us had to come down to earth, and since Werner's preoccupations are so much harder to harness, lying as they do far beyond our galaxy, it fell to me to try and be practical. And try I did, and still do, though often not very successfully, as our daughter, Pia, can attest. She has been our pride and joy from the start, learning to take our inadequacies in her stride while finding her own balance. Later, we learned a great deal from her – and there were times when I honestly do not know what we would have done without her.

We somehow took it for granted that we would stay in Ireland. However, when the moment came for Werner to find a job, we learned to our dismay that there were no openings in that country and Werner was obliged to look further afield. Australia and Canada offered several possibilities and his choice finally fell on the University of Alberta in Edmonton, partly because he recognized the name of a staff member whose area of interest was the same as his own, namely Einstein's theory of relativity. On the map we consulted, Alberta was a friendly light green colour that looked appealing, we thought. Only later did we discover that green is of short duration in that part of the world!

Until we left Ireland we lived on the two scholarships Werner had won from the University of Cape Town, and somehow even managed to send a modest monthly cheque to his mother.

My father lent us the fares to Canada and we very carefully calculated any incidental expenses we might encounter en route. We believed we had thought of everything, but on landing at Dorval in Montreal, we learned that our flight from London did not connect directly with the flight to Edmonton, and were forced to spend a night at a Montreal hotel near the airport, an unexpected expense. To make matters worse, we found out the next morning that the Edmonton flight would leave from a different airport and this transfer by taxi meant another expense. By then, we had practically no money left. Breakfast was out of the question, but perhaps something would be provided on board the plane. I asked the driver of a taxi stationed outside, how much the ride would cost. When he told me, I took out all the unfamiliar Canadian coins we had left and counted them – only to find that we did not have nearly enough. The driver looked at me with a big smile, said "Bienvenue au Canada!" and insisted on taking us, waiving our fare entirely. A lovely welcome!

The next lap of our journey was difficult. The engine of the turbo jet we boarded in Montreal spewed out large flames that shot along-side its wings, as though readying to consume the entire aircraft. Our poor little daughter was terrified. She must have felt that I too worried though I tried hard not to show it. In addition, the flight was quite bumpy and she was airsick a good part of the way. I tried to comfort her while forcing myself to look beyond the flames, and pointed down at the land we were crossing. Canada was a discovery of enormous proportions. We had not thought about this continent in practical terms and were astonished at the hundreds upon hundreds of miles of empty land. Here and there, bodies of water of varying sizes broke the brown monotony. Many hours passed slowly and then, suddenly, Edmonton appeared and we were descending.

People there were very kind. The sense of community was strong. Neighbours soon invited me for coffee to meet other neighbours. At the same time, our arrival there was a culture shock. Walking down Whyte Avenue, felt as if I had stepped into a Hollywood "Western". Only cowboys were missing: on the screen they would have been on horseback, galloping alongside the freight trains we saw when the traffic barriers came down at 104th Street to allow them to pass.

We stared in astonishment at the endless row of box carriages follow one another on the tracks, ending with a caboose – something hitherto unknown to us.

Never could I have imagined before coming here, how disorienting this gigantic landscape can be. The horizon has no boundaries, nor has the sky and the two merge somewhere in the unidentifiable distance. The occasional clouds drifting across the endless expanse of blue were too high to offer the cocooned feeling provided by a typical Irish sky. As for the brown Saskatchewan river, it looked sullen to me with its small rebellious eddies here and there, and bore no resemblance to any other river I had seen.

In Europe, especially in Ireland, people had sung or whistled, not only delivery boys on their bicycles, but anyone anywhere, as they waited on station platforms or walked along the street. Here no one ever sang or whistled, nor was there any birdsong or twitter in the Alberta winter. Only the occasional harsh caw of a magpie broke the weighty silence.

At first we checked into a small motel close to the University. The new term was about to begin and Werner immediately had to sort out his classes, prepare lectures, meet students and so on. Meanwhile, I began to search for an apartment and as soon as I found one, told the owners of the motel, a kind Dutch couple. They asked had our shipment of household things from Ireland arrived yet. When I said no, they insisted on lending us pillows, blankets, cups and plates etc. I promised to return everything as soon as possible and they just nodded and smiled.

It took several weeks for our shipment to arrive and when it did, I immediately set off to return everything we had borrowed. But on reaching that street, I was shocked to find only a hole in the ground where the motel had stood. My first thought was that some disaster had struck, a fire perhaps, but there were no black remnants or ashes. The hollow of what had been the basement of the motel, was perfectly clean. At a nearby store where I asked what had happened, I learned that the motel had been "moved". I still did not understand until it was explained to me that on this continent, whole houses could be moved on a truck.

On our first Saturday evening we took the bus into town. The driver let us off on Jasper Avenue where, in our ignorance, we expected to find a European-type city centre. But none of the buildings had shops with street fronts and as far as we could see, "downtown" boasted only one single restaurant, "The Purple Lantern". Little lights blinked at us from the distance and we walked towards them along Jasper Avenue, believing that this must be where the theatres were, only to find that those lights hung over secondhand car lots. There were no theatres. At the corner of Jasper and 109th Street, a sign pointed North and simply said "Alaska"– nothing else. It felt as if we had stepped into the gaping jaws of emptiness, the night open to an endless depth.

Pia took it all in her stride, quickly adapting to the accent and idiom of other children. She did not mind wearing padded winter clothes and snow boots, and at once took to ice-skating. Werner enjoyed his work and the contact with students, in spite of the extremely heavy teaching load he was given. His surroundings mattered little to him, as I had already discovered in Ireland. On looking up at the stars in Dublin, one unusually cloudless night, it suddenly struck him that no Southern Cross could be seen – this had been his signpost in the sky above Cape Town. By then he had been in Dublin a while, but only at that precise moment, did he fully register the fact that he was in the northern hemisphere now.

In those years city lights did not yet blur the velvety Edmonton night sky teeming with bright, sparkling objects. Its beauty was breathtaking to us both. For Werner, looking at stars and galaxies is also seeing the moments when light left them on its journey to one's eye, with the awareness that looking out into greater distances is also looking further back in time.

Whereas what struck me most was the immensity of that sky and how it dwarfs all that lies beneath it. Never could I have imagined the sense of enormity it conveys, while at the same time revealing one's own insignificance, twirling around as we do on an equally insignificant planet among billions of others. And I asked myself why it should matter so much precisely where one lived on this particular speck dancing to the tune of the universe. But oh! matter it did, dreadfully. It was unreasonable, I recognized that but couldn't help myself: I was homesick for Ireland, for France, for almost any of the many places in Europe where I had lived.

When I received an invitation to a "Faculty Wives' Tea" from the University President's wife, I was overawed, never having met such an exalted person. And how deeply embarrassing when I arrived, to find all the ladies wearing hats and jewelry! I possessed neither. The nametag I was given to pin to my shirt gave only my surname and my husband's faculty, which was mathematics at that time. I wished the tag were big enough to hide me. Someone approached me, bent forward to read it and said, "Mathematics! How fascinating!" I replied that I knew nothing about it, that it was a closed world to me. The President's wife happened to overhear and came to my rescue. She was charming and kind and said, "But my dear, it rubs off! It always rubs off." I could not see what could possibly rub off in this case, but I was grateful to her, especially when she followed this up with telling me how lost she had felt when she and her husband first arrived in Edmonton. The Saskatchewan river, when not hidden by a covering of ice, had looked like a huge dirty gash in the ground to her. However, she had gradually come to like living there. "It takes time!" she said confidently.

In those years, Alberta winters were harsh, with long uninterrupted cold spells. Temperatures did not rise above minus 25 degrees for weeks at a time and often dipped much lower, especially with the wind chill added in. We were doing our best to put down roots when, four months after our arrival in Edmonton, while walking along a downtown street in mid-winter, I had a sudden lung hemorrhage. Old TB lesions had reopened. Until we applied for our Canadian visas and the required X-Rays were taken, I had been quite unaware of ever having been infected myself. On the X-Rays the lesions appeared to have healed, at least sufficiently for me to obtain a temporary visa, which was valid for only six months. Both my husband and little daughter got their immigrant visas without difficulty, but I would be obliged to leave Canada should my health break down within the allotted time.

Fortunately, the University of Alberta, Werner's employer, provided a guarantee that allowed me to be treated and not expelled. This was a promise in words only, not in kind. My actual medical expenses swallowed up practically all of Werner's low beginner's salary, since no medical coverage was granted during the first two years of an immigrant's stay. Yet, somehow, miraculously, we made it. We had to send Pia to my sister who now lived in California, and Werner gave up our rented apartment and moved to a room in one of the student residences. As far as I could tell, he lived on biscuits.

In the Aberhart TB Sanatorium, while on full bed rest, it was a struggle not to feel depressed. My child was over a thousand miles away. I could not even speak to her on the phone. She was in good hands, but still I worried and missed her terribly. The nest we had begun to build was gone. My husband was on his own, snowed under with work.

The patients who were allowed to leave their beds, passed my room in a constant stream, depriving me of all privacy. I asked to have the door shut, but no one would do this for me. There was an unwritten rule that doors remain open as a reminder that we were all in the same boat. After a while, some people began to drop into my room to talk. I learned their histories and personal disasters. One had been brought in immediately after giving birth to her first child, a little boy who was promptly taken away from her. She had barely got a glimpse of him and felt robbed. Some spoke about Shirley, who lay in another room. Her spine was affected by TB, confining her to a striker bed, face down, and this was how she had lain for months. And now her husband had left her for another woman. She did her best to stay cheerful, but on Saturday nights she wept, wanting desperately "to go out on the town". One of the night nurses told me this, a warm, engaging Italian, always in good cheer. In reply to Shirley's outburst she had said, "What? On a Saturday night? Shame on you! That's the most vulgar night of the week!"

There was also Alma, a lady of generous proportions and a generous smile. She was from Georgia and had been at the Aberhart for three years, she told me, before asking me how long I had been "in". When I told her, she said, "Baby, you hasn't even warmed the bed yet! But don't you worry, honey. Sickly folks never dies. They jes' hangs around an' stays sick." She continued to drop into my room also on days when she felt low and at such times, with a scowl on her face, would warn me, "Don't you trust them doctors an' nurses, baby!" But on her good days, she told me risqué jokes, laughing so hard she could hardly get the words out, before ending with, "Ah's jes' as happy as a lark singin' on the fence in the springtime!"

I soon realized that the open-door policy, though it had upset me at first, really worked. It was far better to feel a sense of comradeship with those who were dealing with similar problems than to hide away and lick one's wounds.

The doctor who made the rounds told me that the motto for all TB patients was "Don't stand if you can sit. Don't sit if you can lie down." I spent my time mostly reading. Since local papers carried little international news, Werner brought me the *London Times* and the *Observer*. In my imposed idleness, I read them from cover to cover, including the adverts for theatres, cinemas and art galleries. That was where I found an advert for a London retrospective of Francis Bott's work. I could hardly contain my excitement. Our old friend Francis, the painter! I still had a clear image in my mind of our hotel on the rue des Trois Bornes in Paris, of the room he shared with Manya, of ours on a higher floor, and the life we had lived there together. How those memories suddenly warmed me in my hospital bed! Since leaving Paris just before the war broke out, we had entirely lost touch. Did having a "retrospective" imply that he had died? Or had he become famous? These were burning questions and I quickly put them in writing to the London gallery. It was a very long time before a reply came to say the gallery was not at liberty to answer my questions, but suggested that I address them to a lawyer in Switzerland who was their contact. This I immediately did.

I was long out of the sanatorium and had given up hope of ever hearing back when a letter suddenly came from the Swiss lawyer, but there was no acknowledgement of my letter, nor any mention of my enquiries. He only asked had I any paintings by this artist in my possession as he was compiling a catalogue of his entire oeuvre. Obviously, the works were of some importance now. But why did he not answer my questions? If Francis had died, it would be simple to tell me. His silence implied that Francis was alive. Then why this reluctance to put me in touch with him? I speculated endlessly. Was he ill? Or unable to remember me? Perhaps he wanted to shut out the past? I wrote again but heard nothing further, and had to let the matter rest.

But soon I was able to fly to California to get Pia and bring her back. She told me she was very, very happy to be able to return with me. This was sweet for me to hear but I said, "I thought you were having such a good time here!" With great diplomacy she replied, "Yes, but here is like a luxury hotel. It's not home." I could only hug her.

Happily, we were a family once again and, especially after our son Mark was born, I had little time to think about other things. Now, when asked what I thought of Edmonton, I was able to say, "It's a good place for bringing up children." And I meant it.

Somehow, we all three shared in the excitement of Werner's work, no doubt because we sensed his own enthusiasm for it. Already when they were quite little, both Pia and Mark were intrigued by Werner's preoccupations. On first learning from Werner that he was studying shock waves, Pia asked what they were. Werner's explanation, that they were sound waves produced by a loud noise such as an explosion, quickly prompted her next question, "But how can you study them without hearing the bang?"

The idea that one could study "holes" captivated both children's imagination at a very early age. To amuse them Werner thought up riddles, first for Pia when she was at the right age, then again, years later, for Mark. When Werner asked Pia, "Why is there nothing in holes?" her matter-of-fact answer, "It wouldn't be a hole if there was something in it", has stayed with us ever since. Later, with black holes a favourite topic, she wanted to know: if, as Werner said, a black hole was like a vacuum cleaner that sucks up everything around it, what would happen to a man who was sucked into it? This was the very problem that Werner was probing from a physics point of view – and to this day there are rumblings in the physics community about the possible fate of an observer who falls into a black hole. Children often ask fundamental questions and in this way make us rediscover the world.

Later, Mark invariably prefaced his questions with, "Whappen if...?", too impatient to enunciate every word. In the mornings, on waking before we did, he often came running into our bedroom, tapped Werner urgently on his arm, saying, "Daddy, Daddy, wake up! I feel a question coming!" Their questions grew ever more complex as they matured, especially about the Big Bang that created the universe.

Werner continued to pursue the research that excited him and became more and more distracted. Once as he was leaving for the university, I handed him some envelopes containing cheques and asked him to mail them on his way. It struck me too late that this had probably not been a wise request. When he returned I asked had he remembered to mail them. He thought he probably had. His "probably" prompted my next question, "What colour was the mailbox?" "Green", he said without hesitation. In Ireland the mailboxes had been green. I ran down the street to the next block where there were two dark green boxes. I am not sure what the City of Edmonton kept in them. I searched but found no opening of any kind. Nor were our envelopes lying on top. Presumably some kind person found them and did the neighbourly thing because the payments were not requested a second time.

This was only one of countless such incidents for which Werner soon became well-known to friends and colleagues, who sometimes phoned to ask me was it true that… Physics was an all-absorbing constant, a third presence in our "couple". Once, on a delightful country walk, he suddenly searched his pockets for something to write on but found nothing. He then asked me to search mine but all I could find was a wrapped sweet. The wrapper would be fine, he said. So I threw away the sweet and he scribbled something minute on the wrapper.

Occasionally I find diagrams he has drawn on bits of paper. Many years ago one diagram in particular intrigued me. "Why are you drawing trousers?" I asked. He corrected me: they were not trousers, they were two merging black holes in space-time. Now, following the LIGO detector's miraculous find, this very image is reproduced everywhere in the news media, and when I look at it I see, not two merging black holes, but Werner's trousers dancing to the echo of a billion-year-old chirrup.

The climate did not worry Werner in the least, nor were the winters a problem for the children. Pia, always very active, loved the outdoors at any time of year. Mark delighted in tobogganing with Werner, and no matter how far the mercury dipped, maintained his paper route, often returning with icicles hanging from his eyelashes. As for me, I learned to appreciate the stark and severe beauty of the Rockies and

Canada's amazing wildlife, and stopped looking for Alpine meadows like those in the Swiss or French Alps with their comforting sprinkling of small churches and happy, tinkling cows. When, one winter, a hair grew on my nose, it reassured me: I was as clever at adapting to my surroundings as northern ptarmigans who grow feathers on their feet.

Since our difficult beginning here, all four of us have grown to love Canada deeply. Certainly, Werner quickly developed a sense of belonging and soon felt completely at home, as did the children. It took me a little longer but with time I too began to feel this. In its mosaic pattern, there is a little of everything in this country and so it reflects aspects of many other cultures. Here, one can move freely from one of these to another. This very freedom can be disorienting and frightening at first, as if one were free-floating and had nothing to lean on or hold on to. But the lack of all constraints soon becomes clear and magical, allowing each of us to become who we really are.

Every Canadian city, including Edmonton, offers many opportunities to become acquainted with a large variety of other cultures. When Luisa, a Portuguese acquaintance, invited me to participate in Edmonton's first religious procession to celebrate Our Lady of Fatima, I was delighted to accompany her and discover the local Portuguese community. The people alongside whom I walked were very excited about this initiating festival and it was a pleasure to share in their joy.

Later, Luisa told me that on first arriving in Alberta, she had worked at a chicken processing plant and that many new immigrants worked there before finding other occupations. This prompted me to go to the plant and accept the offer of a tour. I wanted to see how other people earn their living and was surprised at how hard this work was, especially keeping up with the speed at which the assembly lines moved, stopping in front of each worker only very briefly for them to perform the required task.

Before this, I had not given any thought to how such a plant would be operated and it was quite a revelation in many respects. We take so much for granted when we shop for our meals. Suffice it to say, it was a long while before I bought chicken again.

One spring day, while shopping in a downtown department store, I overhead a couple speaking Danish. Without giving it a thought, I greeted them in Danish and we began to chat. It turned out that they were indeed from Denmark and had recently settled in Alberta. Eric was a sheep farmer and he and his wife, Kirsten, also had two children. They told me that the lambing season had just begun and invited me to bring my children to see the new lambs. I did so and we became fast friends, continuing to visit one another for many years.

Claire Harris, a fellow poet, invited me to contribute to an anthology she was co-editing with Edna Alford, *Kitchen Talk,* and I was delighted to accept. A number of friends and acquaintances kindly agreed to let me interview them on the topic of kitchens. All were landed immigrants, each from a different country of origin. My central question was, had kitchens played a pivotal role in their early lives and, if so, how? Some gave fulsome answers with detailed descriptions of life in and around the kitchens of their childhood homes. But two in particular stand out in my memory, both so short as to be terse, but still, so very telling.

Mrs. V., the second last person I interviewed, said she was half Cossack and half Russian. I asked were Cossacks not also Russian, but she denied this vigorously. She too had worked in the chicken processing plant at first. She spoke a mixture of German, Russian and English – peppered with a few choice Italian words learned from her husband, whose boss, in a mattress factory, was Italian. The following were her answers to some of my questions.

Mrs. V. born 1917 (Russia)

We Canada come 1947. Me? Half Russian. Half Cossack.

Kitchen? In *Russia?* In Russia I no cook - work in field all day. Late finish work, dog-tired, just take handful corn, put in mouth, sleep.

Always give husband one spoon turpentine in food. Every day. Is healthy. Is healthy for children too – always 2 drops turpentine in milk when small. Every day. Big men now. Strong. Daughter too. Best have 3 children. If accident with one, two left.

Here, in Canada, have nice house, good kitchen – have everything. Have water. Have big stove. In kitchen no cook on stove - is nice, clean, shiny. Have other stove, in basement. Basement... cook, fry, make cake. Kitchen stay nice, clean.

Daughter married. Big house. Big kitchen. Is happy!

Good husband. He *cook.* He *wash* dishes. He *clean.* Everything!

Son married too. Have job. Have nice house; good kitchen; everything. Is *terrible!*

He cook! *He* wash dishes! *He* clean. Everything! *No good! No right!* Is *man,* son-of-a-gun!

The last person to whom I spoke was in a senior residence. She spoke German and invited me into her room then lay down on her bed. As we chatted, she became more and more animated, half sitting up and gesticulating as she spoke.

Mrs. B. born 1908 (Germany)

Memories of what happened in kitchens?... Well, what can I say? Six I was, in the 1st World War, and only allowed to go to school in the mornings. Afternoons I was sent down the mine. What for? To work, of course! The coal mine. Yes! Filled bucket after bucket with coal. No, it certainly was not easy. It was *hard!* Very hard. But, somehow ...

you go on working. You have to! Not healthy – the air, full of coal, coal dust everywhere. In the ears. In the nose. Inside lungs. But I'm here! *Still*! A little the worse for wear, maybe. But I'm here!

And then, the 2nd World War ... What can I say? War is War.

After that, it's incredible here! When I told them over there that I was going to Canada, they said I was crazy. "What d'you want to go over there for and drink out of their thick glasses?" they asked. But I didn't listen to them. I came. They wouldn't believe how much better it is here – living as the Good Lord himself would in France!

When I arrived, I went to the Immigration Office. There were men and women there of all races and colours - Indian, Chinese, Black - you name it. So I looked up to heaven and I said, "Lord, *this* is your people!"

But in the kitchen? Well, there were pots ... and if there was food, we ate it.

We were very pleased when Werner was invited to Switzerland to spend several months at the University in Bern. The prospect of a stay in Europe was always welcome. I had carefully kept the address of Francis' lawyer and once we were in Bern, I could not resist writing to him again. This time he responded: the answer was yes, Francis was living – and in Lugano! I lost no time in tracking him down and contacting him directly.

LETTER TO FRANCIS

How to begin? Perhaps I will simply do as you asked when you looked at me intently, lifting your glass. "You speak like a poet ..." you said. "When you're back in Canada, write me a story." Here then is the story, Francis. But perhaps you did not want the true one?

When you pronounced those words, I could think of no reply. I had not told you that I wrote poetry or stories. You had not asked me anything – neither about me nor my life.

I had only just found you again – after forty years. You were married now in Switzerland, to Aida, a doctor, you explained as an aside, during introductions at the door and looked at me as though I had fallen from the sky. But you did not seem curious about me, whereas I wanted to find out everything about you, what you had lived through, what sort of man you were. I did not know you. In the distant past I had seen you as a god, not as a man and hardly knew where to begin, but made bold to ask,

"When the war broke out, where were you?"

"Still in Paris ..."

"And you stayed there?"

You answered reluctantly. "Yes. At first I joined up. Later I was in the Maquis, that was the underground movement ..."

"I know, one of my cousins was a member, he was shot ..." You showed no interest in this information and I went on warily, "And Manya?" I was not sure whether it was all right to mention her now, here, in front of your wife. You and Manya had lived together and loved and fought one another in turn.

You looked away and spoke softly, as if you and I were alone.

"She was arrested by the French police under orders of the Gestapo ... She had tremendous courage. She had to have!"

"And then?" I prodded.

Your voice was still low. "She went through a lot ... They tortured her. But she survived, then died in 1960."

When, some hours earlier, you had opened the door to me and let me into your apartment, I had not recognized you. How could I have, after forty years? You kissed me perfunctorily and I felt some embarrassment. I had been so sure that I would always be able to recognize your voice. But even that sounded totally strange already on the phone when I rang you from Bern, then again when you faced me – and you immediately admitted that you did not remember me. Still, I could not give up now. I had dreamed of this meeting for too long.

Aida busied herself putting snacks on the table. She hardly spoke, but observed us quietly, clinically. I was watching your every movement, your little habits, trying to rediscover you. Your face was still young and I searched it for some familiar trait – a look, at least. But nothing about you recalled my great friend of long ago, my god. My hopes dwindled and it felt as if there were a great emptiness around me.

From the armchair where I sat stiffly in your living room, I looked at the paintings on the walls. Suddenly, I was drawn by one of them: an emaciated woman was offering her hollow breast to a dying man. Excited, I exclaimed, "That one is yours! I remember it!" You nodded.

You had been obsessed by the horror scenes that you had witnessed in the Spanish Civil War while fighting alongside volunteers against Franco, and then had painted countless such works. Some of those canvasses, this one included, had haunted me for years.

"It's the only one left of that period."

"And the others?"

You shrugged. "Destroyed during the German occupation."

After the second glass of the Beaujolais I had brought to celebrate this reunion, you were more relaxed. Or perhaps I was. You took me on a tour of all the paintings in your apartment, your own and those by your friends. Then you suggested a walk to your studio. I accepted eagerly. I wanted to see everything, understand everything. Aida did not come with us.

We left the building and took the Via Camara. My attention was divided between you and the splendid panorama stretching out on our left. Your hair was white but no one could have guessed your age. You held yourself very straight and your lithe movements were those of an athlete. My mind jumped back and forth between the Paris of long ago and the Lugano we were walking through now.

"Do you remember our evening walks along the Avenue Parmentier?" I asked, looking at Sorengo Lake which was a dark eye, half-hidden by the surrounding mountains.

"Did we walk there together?" you asked, feeling your way.

"Of course!" I said and noticed Mount Pianbello's peak showing itself flirtatiously between white clouds. "And when my mother or Manya managed to sell one of the hats they made, and we felt rich, we had ice creams on the Place de la République."

"Right!" you said with sudden dawning recognition.

The light turned reddish. The day was failing and trembled with an electric charge to which I too was prey. The sidewalk suddenly came to an end. "We'll have to walk on the road here. But look out for cars!" You said this over your shoulder as you passed ahead with the stride of a young man.

Though the air still held the afternoon heat, I shivered. You were forty years older, but I had just recognized your step! Ignoring the cars, I ran to your side

"On our walks, you often went ahead of me to act the clown or walk like Charlie Chaplin ...

You looked pleased. "And did you like that? Did you laugh?

"Of course! A lot! I loved it!"

For years I had treasured the small watercolour that you made for me as a parting gift when we left Paris. It was with me wherever fate took us. I hung it on the wall where I slept, even when there was no bed to lie in. It was a delicate painting of a young girl in a long white gown who lay in a green field amid wild flowers. I thought it much lovelier than any of your oil paintings.

How long did we stay in your studio? One hour? Two? You opened numerous drawers and, one at a time, you patiently extracted watercolours and drawings. Then, as if it cost you no effort, you placed before me, one by one, innumerable oil paintings of all sizes. I felt a fever rise in you that I, too, caught. The vibrant colours overwhelmed me. The sculpted shapes came off their canvasses. Then, without saying anything, you put the red painting before me. Its dark, almost black outline, contained a centre of the most glowing red I had ever seen. I felt your eyes on me. Although I would have liked to ask you whether it had a name, I dared not say a word. You showed me more, but several times pulled out the red canvas from behind the others to put it before me again – gazing at me intently but still saying nothing.

From then on my eyes returned to it of their own accord. A warmth emanated from it. I wanted to possess that painting, to take it with me and keep it forever, to let it warm me during the long Canadian winters. How beautiful it was! And strong! And true! But I dared not ask you for it. You had just shown me another, commissioned by the Vatican ...

After that you showed me your most recent works. These did not touch me and reminded me of the emptiness I had felt in your apartment where everything was spick and span and so neatly arranged it felt like a doctor's waiting-room. You must have noticed my reaction, because you went through the rest very quickly and then sighed deeply.

"Now I'm tired!"

"I'm not surprised!" We looked at one another and smiled.

As we left your studio, you put your arm around me and pressed me close to you. We walked back slowly to the apartment and Aida, then the three of us went out to dinner.

In the restaurant we made conversation with Aida, then you threw me a mischievous glance and said, "This is certainly different from those cafés of long ago where we had ice creams on 'a good day,' isn't it?"

Those cafés had been sumptuous palaces to me. I did not want you to destroy my memories and defensively said, "Different, yes. But, at that time, even the small hotel where we stayed didn't seem bad ..."

You smiled, remembering. "Ah, yes! The Hôtel de Bretagne ... it had a small bistro ..."

I interrupted, "... where the proprietor's wife let me wash and polish glasses, like a grown-up... There were always people there ..."

"That was where Manya learned to speak French, in that bistro ... I never went back ..."

"I did – about three or four years ago." I babbled on, "I just had to see it all again. It was sad ... dilapidated ... except for my red-brick school across the street. When I went there as a child, it had been quite new. The entrance had a tiled mosaic depicting one of La Fontaine's fables. Its design was the prize-winning entry by one of my sister's classmates at the Lycée Jules-Ferry ..."

I fell silent. You were no longer listening. The Maitre D' was asking you whether you approved of the wine he had chosen for us and whether there would soon be another exhibition of your works.

When he left, you spoke of your work, of the difficult years, of the paintings that would not sell. At night you slaved in Les Halles, the big Paris Market, carrying large sacks of vegetables and potatoes. During the day you looked after Manya, who was left paralysed after her ordeal. She could no longer walk and you carried her everywhere. In addition there was a little girl, Manya's niece, whose parents had been deported to one of the death camps. She was only four years old. You took care of her.

I looked at you, listened to you. Little by little, as you spoke, I recognized your mouth, your lips, your teeth. This was how I had watched you long ago – while you spoke. You used to come up to our room to talk politics or literature, to read poetry to us ...

There was a moment's silence and I said, "In the evenings you often came up to our room. You read us poems by Rilke ... I couldn't understand them but felt they were infinitely beautiful ... because you read them."

"Were you three girls?"

Were we – my mother, my sister and myself – three girls in your vague memories? My mother, whom events had separated from my father for several long years, felt abandoned in Paris. Though you were some years younger, you were the only man she really talked to ... She looked up to you: you were well-read, courageous, idealistic. As for my sister, in her early teens then, you must have been the first man in her life.

And to me, you were a father figure, a close friend – a god ... We all three loved you. Aloud I said, "There were my mother, my sister and I. We probably spoke German together ... Sometimes Manya would let slip something in Czech and my mother would reply in Russian ... Do you remember the others in the hotel? The Polish tailor with two sons? The Spaniard with one arm who typed a clandestine paper at night? And Lisbeth who couldn't speak without swearing and pasted reminders to herself on the wall of her room saying, "NICHT FLUCHEN!" and "Halt's Maul!" ("No cursing!", "Shut your trap!")

Aida looked put out. She didn't speak German. I felt guilty, but to translate those few words for her would have been condescending. She left the table to go to the ladies' room. Perhaps she was simply bored. Or did she resent all this talk of a distant past in which she had played no part?

You seemed not to notice as you concentrated. "The Spaniard, yes ... But not the others."

"You and Manya used to sing duets from Don Giovanni ..."

You brightened. In a low voice, you intonated, "Reich mir die Hand, mein Leben, und komm in mein Schloss mit mir ..." ("Give me your hand, my love, and come with me to my castle ...")

I leaned toward you. "Yes, yes! That's what you sang, holding hands! At other times, Manya and my mother sang Russian songs together ..."

"She had a good voice, Manya," you said.

"I remember. It was rich and full ... My mother too ..."

You cut in, "She made hats. That's what we lived on."

"I know", I said. "My mother too. They had both taken the same millinery course sponsored by a committee for refugees. But my mother always said Manya had more of a flair than she had."

"Yes, she had talent, Manya."

I didn't tell you that I also clearly recalled your quarrels, when Manya threw things at you. Once she hit you on the head with her iron. You fled up to our room and my mother put cold compresses on your head. Nor did I tell you that I clearly remembered the bad times, when Manya did not manage to sell her hats and went out in the evenings to sell herself. At the time, I had no idea what this meant. Only years later did I understand. And once I did, I looked with new eyes at your painting of the girl in a white gown, so low-cut that her young breasts showed, with pink nipples matching the snout of the little mouse you had put in one corner. I have never been quite sure whether the little painting then disappeared by accident during one of our many moves, or whether I lost it on purpose after I understood what Manya had "sold" – obviously with your approval.

You lowered your eyes before speaking again. "I didn't want to live after she died. Nothing mattered any more. I no longer cared about anything. I was rich by then, very rich. I began to drink. I drank up nearly everything. I wanted to put an end to it ..."

Deep pain showed clearly on your face and made you pause. Then, frowning, you continued. "Her death was extraordinary. She felt that she was going to die. Do you know what she said to me? We were in the car. Suddenly she said, 'For thirty years I carried you in my belly. Now you're going to be born.' Those were her last words. She fell into a coma and never woke again ..."

I forgave you. I forgave you for everything.

We remained silent for a time. Then, very gently, the emptiness filled. You took my hand. Your voice, too, was gentle when you said,

"I'm so very happy to have found my little friend of long ago. So very, very happy!"

"So am I! You'll never know!" Again I used the formal 'vous'.

You noticed. "No, no! Don't say 'vous' any more! Didn't you say 'tu' to me long ago?"

"Probably ..." I faltered, suddenly shy.

"Well, then! ... Don't say 'vous' to your old friend! Ah! I'm so happy to have you here!"

"I am too. I'll never be able to tell you ..." I stopped. I was saying 'vous' again! Quickly, I corrected myself.

In a different tone of voice you said, "Your eyes ... they're beautiful! Very beautiful!"

I was surprised to find myself blushing.

Outside the restaurant, I did not feel the freshness of the night. Thousands of lights danced in the lake. The palm trees stretched upwards to touch the stars.

My train was due to leave shortly. We drove to the station and when we arrived there I said my goodbyes to Aida and shook her hand. She smiled, staying in the driver's seat, but you got out. You closed the car door and took me in your arms. With tears in your eyes, you kissed me. You held me close, very close ... and your embrace and my response became the red painting for me to take back to the long Canadian winters.

In a suddenly low confidential voice, you said that you had a second studio in Montparnasse in Paris.

"Really?" I asked, not listening properly, too intent on the moment.

But then you whispered in my ear, "I often go to Paris. Alone. Come to me there ..."

DISCOVERIES

In the years that followed, Werner's work took us abroad more and more frequently. Once, on an extended stay in Paris in the 1970s, we rented the upper storey of a house on the rue Jean Dolent, not far from the Institut Henri Poincaré, where Werner would spend his days. The street was reassuringly quiet when I went to view the property and to my surprise, so was the rear, in spite of the métro line running above ground on this section of Boulevard Saint Jacques, which flanked the back garden.

The house was at least 150 years old and its well preserved interior greatly appealed to me. The rooms with their overhead beams and sloping floorboards were reminiscent of Van Gogh paintings. The landlord, who was about to leave Paris for a time, showed me around. Then, as he handed me the keys, he pointed to the house next door and said, "The Irishman, Samuel Beckett, lives there." Beckett, by then, was a cult figure and a legend. I felt stunned and could only enquire lamely, "You know him?"

"Oh, we greet one another," he said with a wave of his hand.

Beckett's writing had puzzled and fascinated me since my teens, and so had the man. Everything about him was contradictory. He was brought up by a devoutly Protestant mother in a country ruled by the Catholic Church; he was devoted to her but until mid-life, struggled to free himself of her; he loved the King James Bible but did not believe in it. He loved Ireland but left to live in France. He had a deep urge to write but despaired of language being able to express anything meaningful. His appearance was severe, even forbidding, yet he was the kindest, most generous of men.

Once in a Dublin court of law, appearing as a witness in defence of an uncle charged with libel, Beckett had to state whether he was a Christian, a Jew or an atheist. He replied, "None of the three!" Perhaps he was echoing a favourite Irish saying, "It takes all kinds to make up the world and thank God we're none of them!"

Our paths never actually crossed, but they had often been similar, since his two countries, Ireland and France, were also two of mine. In Ireland, unknowingly, I roamed in the same areas where he had wandered, along the same stretch of coast and in the Dublin mountains. And now, in Paris, he lived in the house next door!

"Do you see him often?" I asked the landlord.

"Not really, he goes away for months at a time", he said.

A second surprise followed when we were settling in on the upper floor. I drew back the curtains, opened a window wide and only then discovered that we were facing a prison.

I had failed to notice it from the narrow street because of the high wall surrounding it, and only now did I realize why a policeman was stationed in a booth at the corner. From our first floor window, this prison was clearly visible and of course the view cut both ways. On seeing me looking out, one of the inmates, his face glued to a barred window, called over at once, "Madame, quelle heure est-t-il?" Too startled to reply, I hurriedly closed the window and carefully drew the curtains.

Later I learned that he had not really asked me for the time. According to Jean Genet, a writer who spent a certain amount of time behind bars himself, there is a whole prison code based on different hours of the clock. I was left to guess what "my" prisoner had meant.

In the mornings, lorries drove the convicts off to work and all was calm. But no sooner did they return in the afternoon than we heard them clearly, especially on summer evenings, when the oppressive heat added to their restlessness. They hurled colourful curses from window to window, calling one another names, each trying to top the last. "Fils de pute!" (Son of a whore!), would at once elicit a stronger retort, "Fils d'un chameau et d'une pute!" (Son of a camel and a whore) and on. They also chanted or sang, beating time with hard objects on the bars. Some, obviously pimps, carried on a shouted conversation with their "poules", who gathered on the street below. The little slang I knew was not sufficient for me to understand most of what they said, and my argot dictionary, compiled by a former police officer, was no help. Slang changes constantly and this dictionary, though recent, was already out of date.

One evening after we had gone out, some friends called to see us. They rang our doorbell and immediately, one of the prisoners called down to them, "Ils sont sortis. Vous n'avez qu'à nous demander. C'est NOUS les concierges!" (They've gone out! You can just ask us. We're the concierges.)

It turned out that this was the Prison de la Santé, one of the three most important prisons in France, housing not only minor offenders but also hardened criminals and political detainees. Somewhere on the far side of that wall was a guillotine, still used in the early 1970's.

The front of Beckett's house faced in the opposite direction from ours, out toward Boulevard Saint Jacques. But from his studio he had the same view as we had of the prison, with its inmates behind barred windows; he too could hear their raucous shouts, their swearing and singing. When someone asked him once did he not find all this very disturbing, he admitted that he did. But he stayed on in that house. Another friend once saw him use a flashlight to exchange Morse code signals with one of the prisoners.

With all this in mind, it struck me as strange that Beckett had never portrayed a prison nor even alluded to one in any play or other work. Surely, I thought, another writer would have taken advantage of this setting so conveniently offered on his very doorstep. But why had

Beckett chosen to live in this location in the first place? It cannot be a coincidence that prisoners everywhere, from prisons in Germany to San Quentin in California, are interested in Beckett's plays, especially in "Waiting for Godot", either as entertainment, or to act in themselves. Beckett himself helped some of them with their productions, even rehearsing with them.

But perhaps he did not need to use a prison setting. Imprisonment is implicit in all his work, portrayed in his cryptic fashion. Everyone of his characters is a prisoner of some kind, buried up to their neck in sand, stuffed into garbage cans or dominated by a voice from the past.

The public at large may look on "Waiting for Godot" as an unanswered riddle, but prisoners everywhere understand it viscerally. They know what it is to wait and wait. They identify with the characters and their miserable existence. Their search is universal: to find meaning.

I stared at Beckett's house, keenly aware of his virtual presence and speculated endlessly about the man, his motives and his writing. During the German occupation of France, Beckett joined the Résistance. Later, he shrugged it off as having been "Boy Scout stuff", but he was in fact an active agent of his "cell", Gloria SMH, of whose eighty members only twenty survived. The other sixty were denounced to the Gestapo by a priest, the abbé Robert Alesch, who had infiltrated Gloria, pretending to be a sympathizer. In reality he was a highly paid collaborator who received a bonus for every activist he denounced to the "Abwehr", a German Intelligence Network. The victims were then arrested by the French police under orders from the Gestapo, held in this very prison, the Prison de la Santé or in the Prison de Fresnes, and interrogated under torture by the German police before being deported to one of the death camps. Beckett's close friend, Alfred Péron, was one of the first of the Gloria members to be arrested by the Gestapo, held in the Prison de la Santé and subsequently deported.

At the end of the war, Alesch, while fleeing towards Belgium, was caught and held in this same prison prior to being executed.

Looking across the street, I wondered what strangely contradictory feelings must have coursed through Beckett while he looked at the very building in which several of his friends had been interrogated under torture before being assassinated and which, subsequently, also held the man responsible for their fate, before he in his turn was executed.

Was it a constant reminder of the ultimate absurdity of life – the central theme of all Samuel Beckett's work?

WIDENING THE CIRCLE

Werner's research interests soon led to his becoming acquainted with colleagues all over the world, scientists who work in the area of physics and cosmology that make up his own spiritual home. It has been a privilege and a joy for me to become part of this large community, and to be able to count among our closest friends some who became famous but have remained modest and approachable, including former students. It is both wonderful and warming to know they are there, within phone and email reach, like a family-at-large.

Among the most inspiring in the sphere of courage and determination are Jane and Stephen Hawking. We first met in 1971, when Werner was invited to spend some time in Cambridge. Becoming better acquainted with both on each of our return visits, we were soon good friends, especially after our year in California when Werner and Stephen were invited to Caltech at the same time.

Stephen's ability to focus on his work, the superhuman strength of character it takes to do this even as his body gradually deteriorates, his readiness to address the difficulties and problems of others while never discussing his own, all these attributes are legendary. And Jane is equally remarkable. Always welcoming and generous, she makes her friends feel at home, while at the same time looking after her family. This was a juggling act that never ceased to amaze me, especially when the children were little and Stephen's needs already on the increase. At that time there were not yet any nurses in the picture to help, only an occasional graduate student or post-doctoral fellow of Stephen's who would lend a hand. Jane was there, was everywhere. The children were never neglected, nor was Stephen, nor were her many friends. She helped countless post-doctoral fellows and colleagues and their wives among the constant flow of visitors to Cambridge. She shopped and cooked, did her washing and hung up diapers to dry; stretched netting over raspberry bushes to protect the fruit; entertained; and in addition to all this, she somehow studied French, and earned a Ph.D.

We have wonderful memories of delicious lunches at their home on West Road, prepared single-handedly by Jane. At the table, after serving everyone, she would feed Stephen as if it were the most natural thing in the world, while carrying on a perfectly normal conversation. Then followed a game of croquet on the lawn or an afternoon of music when Jane would sing and her father accompany her on the piano.

I still see Stephen whizzing round the garden, giving the children rides on his wheelchair which he manœuvred with skill and great care for the children's sake. But on his own, he disregarded all pleas to take it slowly – absolutely refusing to do so, even at dangerous road crossings. He did, in fact, have more than one accident at the latter, but still did not slow down. Werner well remembers an occasion when Jane drove him and Stephen up to London to a meeting of the Royal Society. Once Stephen and his wheelchair were deposited on the side-walk, there was no holding him back. He chased along at such speed that Werner felt obliged to run ahead of him, waving his arms wildly at pedestrians and calling, "Watch out for the wheelchair!"

Notwithstanding his many problems, Stephen had the great kindness to take our son to see the first Star Wars film, while Mark was alone in England, living in a Cambridge boarding-school. And many years later, when Stephen learned that Mark was confined to a wheelchair and, like himself, unable to speak, he lost no time in writing to us with suggestions of how we might help Mark.

STINTS AS PERFORMERS

We returned to Switzerland several times for longish periods and happened to be based in Bern when Einstein's old apartment was opened as a Museum. This was where he and his first wife Mileva had lived. There was next to nothing on display as yet and the curator and I began to chat. He told me that Einstein's papers had just been opened to the public, after a fifty-year moratorium. From private letters among these, it emerged that Einstein and Mileva had had a child before they were married, a child whose existence had never been acknowledged; who had never been mentioned in the many accounts of Einstein's life; for whom no entry could be found in any birth or death register; a child who had simply disappeared.

I began to dig. Little "Lieserl" had certainly existed. The letters leave no doubt. She was born in 1902. (And thirty years later, when a thirty-year-old woman approached Einstein, claiming to be his daughter, he did not dismiss the matter out of hand, but hired a private detective to find out who this person was.)

Einstein's parents opposed their son's marriage to Mileva, convinced that it would ruin his every chance of success both academically and socially. They did not relent even when Mileva became pregnant in 1901, and she returned to her parents to give birth. Then, a year later in 1903, Albert's father, on his death-bed, reluctantly agreed to the marriage. His mother never became reconciled to the union nor did she ever acknowledge her two grandsons born later. Lieserl was not mentioned again.

Born in 1875 of Serb parents in Titel (then Hungary), Mileva at age twenty traveled alone to Switzerland – a country where, at that time, foreigners were not easily accepted – to enroll in the Faculty of Mathematics and Physics at the ETH in Zürich, a Technical College where women were still very much looked down on. She took the same courses as Einstein, and was only the fifth woman ever to enroll in this Faculty, which was regarded as male territory, and in that year she was the only one. Physically she suffered from a deformity of the hip due to a congenital disease that caused her to limp. She also believed herself to be very ugly.

I could not help but feel sympathy for her. Why, I wondered, in the many biographies of Einstein written before 1987, was Mileva – if mentioned at all – dismissed in a sentence or two? Her Ph.D. thesis was rejected by her supervisors at the ETH and she was not granted a doctorate. Because of her pregnancy and the circumstances surrounding it? Or was she treated unfairly by her superiors, as some accounts hint? She herself was convinced of the latter.

Having gathered all available facts, I had a strong image of Mileva and of her relationship with Albert that somehow rang true. All this then found its way into a fictitious – but based on fact – dialogue I wrote, portraying the couple. After it was broadcast on Radio Canada, Werner and I gave readings of this script in many places across the world.

We both enjoyed these thespian stints – Werner was a "natural" and quite pleased on one occasion at being taken for a professional actor. He wore a wig for the role and certainly made a wonderful Einstein. Our very first "gig" was in Japan, where we were spending a year. It all came about when one of the physicists at the Yukawa Institute of Physics in Kyoto, invited me to give a poetry reading there. I was filled with doubt. I could not imagine an audience consisting of only physicists wanting to hear my reading and said so to my host. He waved this away, saying, "It will be good for them!" which did not allay my apprehension. I then decided to substitute the Einstein dialogue for poetry. The subject matter at least, would be more relevant, I thought. To my immense relief Werner, being a good sport, agreed to do this with me, but I told no one in advance that he would.

Our next daunting challenge was finding an "Einstein" wig in Kyoto. A friend drove me to every possible place in the city in search of one, but all available wigs were intended for the Noh theatre – enormous, jet black and unruly affairs, as required by tradition for this ancient art. We were about to give up when I spotted one that was only chin-length and not black – it was a pale blond. I decided it would have to do and ruffled it as best I could.

And so, after introducing myself to the unexpectedly large audience, I said that I had a surprise in store for everyone, namely a very famous guest who had just arrived. At this cue, Werner came into the hall wearing the pale blond wig, put on a thick German accent and said, "Ach, das ist ja wunderbar to be back in Kyoto! …" (Einstein had actually been there in 1922). No one among his colleagues recognized him for quite a few moments and it was plain sailing from there.

Discovering Japanese culture was exciting and enriching. Some aspects of it appealed to me profoundly. One of the many special moments I took away with me, was of a priest in a temple garden who pointed out how beautiful a single flower looks, whereas a bed full of flowers cannot be appreciated in the same way. How true this is, of many things. I was also drawn to the concept of *Wabi-sabi*, an aesthetic that favours the asymmetry of organic forms and the impermanence of natural materials. It emphasizes the beauty of "subtle imperfection", as in a handmade tea bowl. I especially loved the reverence for simplicity – although I am aware of the paradoxically complicated steps often taken to achieve such an effect.

Japan, its people and culture cast a very special spell that I could still feel even after we had boarded our aircraft for the return flight to Canada. I sat in my seat, my head still full of images that I desperately tried to retain while finishing a poem I had begun to write in Kyoto, "The last Samurai". It was part of a collection I had written during our year in Kyoto. To my dismay, our flight landed before I could complete it. Afraid the spell would break the instant I stepped outside or spoke to anyone, I scurried into a deserted corner of the arrivals lounge, sat down and wrote the last lines. Only then did I dare look at the Canadian scene before me.

Happily, we are still in touch with many dear friends in Japan, who made us feel welcome in their country and were wonderfully patient with us and our clumsy foreignness.

IN SEARCH OF ROOTS

Naturally, my mother's vivid depictions of her country and its people, her love for its literature, its music, and the songs she sang in her emotive contralto, had all made an indelible impression on me. And so when Werner was invited to St. Petersburg in 1990, I was thrilled to be able to go with him.

On our arrival, hearing the language that I did not understand, but whose intonations and inflections I knew so well, made me feel hopeful of finding my mother's roots.

After only a day or two in Moscow, we took the night train to St. Petersburg. The Iron Curtain was just then beginning to lift, but clearly this did not yet apply to the ban on looking out of train windows – these were tightly covered with layers of some indeterminate material that would not budge. I worked hard at peeling back at least a small corner and managed to do so, but it did not yield far enough for me to get more than a passing glimpse of an old cabin here, or a shriveled tree there.

Dreamily swaying with the motion of the train, I sat in the dimly lit carriage, aware of the legendary steppes somewhere ahead, of their enormity under a sky that offers no perspective. I thought not only about my parents' three-month journey across this region in 1918, but especially of my father's trek to Siberia four years earlier as a prisoner-of-war. With my mind's eye I suddenly saw his tousled, eighteen year-old head among the sea of others on their way to the internment camp, marching or being transported through this unknowable vastness. I felt very close to him there, sensed his apprehension and wanted to reach out and touch him, to whisper that it would be alright, he would be safe.

The next morning it was exciting to arrive in St. Petersburg, the centre of so many pivotal events and where some of the great figures whom my mother held in high esteem, had lived: Feodor Chaliapin, the world-famous bass, in whose old apartment still hangs a painting that cracked spontaneously in 1938, supposedly when this celebrated singer died in Paris; Pushkin, author of *Eugene Onegin* and *Boris Gudonov*, who had lived here in a once magnificent mansion, until he died at only thirty-seven in an ignoble duel; Shostakovitch, whose music speaks for so many, lived in twenty different apartments in this city. I made my way to the Neva river, remembering Raskolnikov's mental anguish as he walked here in *Crime and Punishment*; I visited the prison where Dostoyevsky survived his infamous fake execution before being sent into a ten-year exile.

Werner's colleagues and their families were kindness itself. We were taken to see the famous Kirov Ballet and to hear a wonderful concert, appreciating them all the more because we knew that obtaining tickets to these events was fiendishly difficult at that time. We were invited to the homes of people with whom we became good friends, and were offered delicious meals that had clearly been planned well in advance – we knew they must have stood in line for hours on preceding days at grocery shops for precious foods. But outside this welcoming circle of people we saw no one smile. The general manner and facial expression of everyone we encountered was dour and mistrustful.

Mikhail Gorbachev was, at that time, beginning to open political doors and windows and we had expected people to be jubilant about the historic changes being introduced. Instead, we were struck by a general feeling of doom and foreboding. No one trusted Gorbachev, no one believed that the changes he was introducing would be for the better.

Artists, sitting or standing at their easels on designated streets, were the first visible buds of free enterprise. They had been forbidden to do this under the Soviet Regime. The sudden change was still so new that, instead of being happy and relaxed, they looked self-conscious and uncomfortable. I wandered into a church where a service was in progress – one of the first to be held officially since the ban on the practice of religion was lifted after several decades. The people I saw gathered there, were mostly old women with a longing in their eyes. A tour guide brought in a group of tourists and her raucous voice rose well above the priest's prayers as she reeled off the history of the church and details of its architecture. Twice the priest interrupted his prayers and politely asked her to speak more softly, but she pretended deafness.

When a group of us were taken to visit Catherine's Palace, a woman guard at the entrance to the grounds refused to unlock the gate. She spoke rapidly in deep anger, on and on, while we stood and waited. Someone explained to us that the guard was upset at our coming here without having any idea of the hardship, the hunger, the cold and suffering that Russian people had had to endure during the war, during the terrible siege of Leningrad; that we knew nothing of the hundreds of thousands who had perished; that, in our ignorance, we were thoughtlessly visiting magnificent treasures which had been restored thanks to untold sacrifices. And so on. It took a very long time before she finally fell silent and grudgingly opened the gate for us.

Inside Catherine's Palace, our shoes covered by large felt slippers, we climbed marble stairs then shuffled around under crystal chandeliers enclosed by gold-leaf-covered walls, as out-of-place as my mother would have felt had she lived to return there. Her quaking presence filled a vacuum beside me as I padded across precious inlaid floors where Catherine the Great once trod beside the husband she soon had imprisoned; the same Catherine whose little embalmed finger was carried more than a century later at the forefront of processions, followed by throngs of people squabbling to be closest to the front, closest to the cherished finger, and my mother, a small girl straining to see, asked "What is so special about a finger?" That was before she found out about fingers and hands and salutes.

Back outside, I tried hard to make eye contact with people, especially with the elderly, wanted so much to reach out to them. It seemed very important to find some element, some spark of all that my mother had loved and admired. But I could not. Nor could I, try as I might, picture my mother among the people I met and saw. She no doubt changed after leaving her homeland, but so had everyone here. The entire country was undergoing a metamorphosis at that very moment, the second one in the span of time since my mother left.

I watched the grey water of the Neva flow past and thought about the Russian culture – ever-wounded, ever-shifting and chaotic, ever worshipful of an icon before overthrowing it for the next. I used to look at the Saskatchewan river when spring came to Edmonton, and try to imagine those far away rivers in the Russian springs of my mother's memories, when birds return, silent at first, their song still frozen; when snow and ice become unsafe as hollows suddenly appear where before, all was solid. I could still hear her voice describe the muffled pings and clinks of sparkling ice blocks stubbing and shoving one another on their way forward to freedom, sounds as nostalgic as the liquid phrase of a balalaika.

Memories have an inherent beauty and truth of their own.

Note: *Mikhail Gorbachev has received numerous awards including the 1990 Nobel Peace Prize. Most recently, in 2012, he was given the new Carl Friedrich von Weizsaecker Award in Germany for "solving conflicts while avoiding the use of force" and for "accepting responsibility for his acts". The acts for which he accepted responsibility were those of bringing about changes "too quickly". In his own country, he was never given credit for what he tried to achieve, opposed not only by the communists whose regime he dismantled, but also by its opponents.*

A year after our visit to St Petersburg, I learned that my older sister was flying back to Ireland. I wanted to accompany her, but she asked me not to do so, and sisterly intuition failed to guide me, although I knew that she had cancer.

Only later did I learn that she had gone to Ireland to be with her daughter there on learning that she was terminally ill. At this I immediately flew there, but she was already in a hospice.

SISTERS

There's a knock on the door. I open it. One of them stands there smiling. His right hand holds out a hot water bottle to me. "Put that in your bed, then sip this slowly and you'll be alright." His left hand holds up a brandy glass. It's full. "It's not the cold at all, you see. It's the shock", he says as he walks boldly into the room.

Surely, he shouldn't be coming in. True, he belongs in this house in a way I do not, for I'm not of the faith. In fact, there's no reason why I should have been admitted or allowed to stay here. Still, I was given this guest room out of kindness, because my sister lies in a coma in a nearby hospice and, for the time being, it is mine. My private room. Am I imagining things? Is he simply expansive in his eagerness to help? Meting out solace and understanding is his profession. He is a man of God, although not mine. It is, must be, a lonely profession, practiced largely in isolation. Can he be faulted for wanting momentary contact? I take the hot water bottle and press it to my chest, still shivering.

"Put that into your bed now, then get in and sip this." He penetrates further into the room and places the glass of brandy next to the telephone on the bedside table. It glows amber under the lamp. Murmuring my thanks, I lift the blankets as little as possible. To lift them higher is out of the question in his presence. I slip the hot water bottle under them, repeat my thanks and wait for him to go. Is his lingering simply kindness? I'm being ridiculous! His temples are greying. Mine are too. There can be nothing behind his gesture.

But he takes my hand in both of his. "It's the shock, you see." His middle finger, first pressing into the hollow of my palm, now extends hard and firm along my wrist.

My mind leaps to another man in another house, long ago in a different country, who took us in. The one whom we trusted implicitly, who appeared to be kind, fed us, promised to look after us. For a lifetime I've been careful not to voice these leaps of the mind to my sister. She doesn't want to hear of them, speak of them, remember. She has trained her thoughts to follow a forward linear path. If something or someone causes them to deviate, she gets very angry.

I try to feel my sister's anger. Once more I repeat my thanks, try to withdraw my hand, take a pace back. He doesn't move and his face betrays nothing, has not betrayed anything from the start. I pull my hand free. Only then does he wish me a drawn-out goodnight and leave. I close the door behind him, lean against it.

My sister would not have thanked him. Certainly not three times. She would have cut him off faster, more decisively. She would have blocked his entry into the room. Many years ago she learned a lesson, one I never mastered. She would have anticipated his moves, not been surprised by them. Only outraged anew. No, not anew. Outraged as always, her outrage two-pronged, one prong a driving force, the other doubled-back, making her turn away.

I don't know how to turn away.

Today I was quite sure I'd found my sister, the one I longed for. I could touch her, feel her, hear her breathe. I hesitated to throw my arms around her, not sure that a hug from me would be welcome. I didn't want to violate the barrier she had set up between us. But all at once I did. I took her in my arms. I couldn't help myself.

It was then I had the shock. She suddenly opened her eyes and they were the eyes of a stranger. Did she not recognize me? Or was it I who did not recognize her? Ever since I can remember, people have mistaken me for my sister. Yet we're not alike. She is dark and I am fair. Her eyes are brown and mine grey. It's difficult to understand how I could be mistaken for her. The opposite can't possibly be true. No one could mistake her for me. She has a scholarly mind. And pride. I've never possessed either. Her judgments are instant. Mine meander, for nothing ever seems wholly good or wholly bad.

The first time my sister and I were to meet again after events and borders had separated us for what seemed like a very long time, I was terribly excited. My mother had fetched me from Belgium and brought me to a large house in Sèvres. Now my sister too would come there from Strasbourg where other relatives had taken her. The garden surrounding the house seemed as big as a park. The trees had golden crowns. Fallen leaves formed an ankle-deep yellow carpet for her to swish and crunch her way through. I was careful not to disturb it, to leave it intact for her. Mahogany chestnuts, fresh out of their spiked green shells, waited for her. To spare her the trouble of looking for them, I gathered them, counted and polished them, watched over them to make sure they wouldn't turn a dull, dry dark before she arrived. Perhaps her journey would make her hungry. I took some caramels from a tin, softened them on top of the radiator and made them into shapes for her.

Then I became a chestnut and lay in wait, my ear to the ground, listening for her. At the sound of her approach, I half-closed my eyes and watched. She didn't come running. She was a queen walking slowly down the path towards me, and then stepped over me. She looked much bigger and older. The chestnuts held no interest for her. She looked disgusted at the caramel braids and pretzels. I cried. I cried for the sister she was not. And she – what did she wish I were?

Or was she terribly excited at the prospect of seeing me again – her little sister? Did she hurry along the path to me, only to find my arms were not outstretched in welcome? Did I lie on the ground ignoring her, pretending not to care whether she was there or not? Would she ever forgive me?

How did forgiveness work? Only certain people possessed it and could bestow it on others. Asking for it was useless. But if one managed to acquire some, could one pass it on to someone else? The answer eluded me.

Our secret language contained no words such as "forgiveness". It was to us what NUSHU had been to women in ancient China – a language invented by them, used to communicate their innermost secrets to one another. They transcribed it in characters that represented sounds instead of meanings. NUSHU booklets and songs were traditional gifts between women as they gathered together to sing the songs.

It gave them a powerful feeling of sisterhood. Men, suspicious of NUSHU, called it the "witches' script".

Our language, too, consisted of sounds instead of words and gave us a sense of strength in sisterhood. When we spoke it, we wore the expressions of others, adopted their mannerisms, mimicked their voices, pretended we were saying meaningful things to one another. Language and speech reveal what one is. We had no native tongue in the true sense and had become linguistic chameleons with conditioned reflexes, unconsciously changing as the need arose. Sometimes we pretended ignorance of this or that language until we were sure we could trust the people who spoke it. We had also learned that with each language comes a different built-in philosophy. And prejudices.

This switching from one way of speaking to another made everything I said sound tentative. I envied birds their easy fluid song – they were never in doubt about the next note. I envied my sister's mastery of grammar and vocabulary in several languages. She never tired of correcting mistakes. She wanted to elevate all thought, speech and writing, to make it error-free. She, the rationalist, wanted the world to be perfect. And I, the dreamer, knew it could never be.

There's no change. My sister is still in a coma. Before and after hospice visits, I follow trails we trod together. Retracing our steps of long ago may help me find the key to what we once had. In terms of months, years, this is where we stayed together longest. The memories of it are among the many I carry with me, but cannot voice to my sister for fear of making her angry. There were happy times here, but those too she drowns in her anger.

They know about my sister at this house. They sympathize. Word has spread. I have hardly spoken to anyone. But everyone knows everything immediately. It is uncanny in a house where carpets muffle footsteps, doors close silently and voices are subdued. Do they also know of his knocking on my door? Had he got the brandy and hot water bottle from the kitchen? If so, he must have been seen. But perhaps he had not revealed his intentions and no one knew where he took them.

Or do they know of his stepping into my room? It cannot be acceptable behaviour. Of that I am sure, although I don't see things in black and white as they do. As they must, according to their beliefs.

My sister had no such beliefs, but she too, had a clear picture of right and wrong. For her no overlap, no confusing borderline situations blurred the issues. I admired and feared the clarity of her vision. It was as if she were looking through a magnifying glass that boldly defined boundaries quite invisible to me.

It's my first evening here and I'm anxious to go to bed as quickly as possible, so as to make an early start the next morning. The feeling of urgency is strong. What if I find my sister too late?

I have a restless night, sleeping and dreaming fitfully. She is there, at the foot of the bed, much larger than life.

I jump out and try to reach her, stretch out my arms toward her but cannot come closer. I am in water up to my chin, struggling forward with all my strength but masses of seaweed catch my legs. I call out her name.

She is angry and says, "I told you not to come!"

I try to laugh it off, "It was now or never!" The remark is made in all innocence. No dark undertone was intended. But, as soon as the words are out, I realize their full implication.

"Don't say that!" she cries out. "Don't say it!"

I didn't mean that this was the end, but there is no way of unsaying it.

She, too, woke up trembling once – she'd seen me fall down a flight of stairs in her dream and feared for my life. That very night I had fallen down a staircase. It was a measure of our closeness. This is my second evening. I have come in after a day of searching. Mary who always sits in the front lobby, looks up when I open the heavy front door and asks, "Any luck with your search today?"

She does not really understand what I am searching for.

Do I?

I shrug and she hangs her head, "Ah, it's very hard on you!" She goes to the kitchen at once and I hear her ask them to make a nice cup of hot tea for me. I quickly go up to my room to take off my coat and wash my hands. One of them passes me on the stairs.

He smiles, "Well now, any luck today?" So he, too, knows of my search. I shake my head but he goes on smiling. "Ah, you're bound to have some one of these days."

"I don't know", I whisper.

"Never say die!" he calls after me.

The word makes me shudder. I will not entertain it in my thoughts. It's different for him. He isn't really touched by this. Besides, dying and death are among his daily concerns, events at which he performs rituals and offers comfort. But I don't count among his lambs.

In bed, I'm afraid of falling asleep. There might be another knock at the door. If I'm asleep I may not hear it. Whoever it is might come in then. Without my knowing. But he could also come in without knocking. The door isn't locked. There's no key or bolt. Not in this house. I wouldn't be able to shout. This is not a house one shouts in. Even if it were, I wouldn't be able to. At such times my voice fails me as if I were born without vocal chords.

I could get up and angle a chairback under the door handle. But that's not done in this house any more than shouting. The doors and walls muffle all sound, they are made of cotton wool, give way when touched. The floor too. I sink deeper and deeper under my own weight. My body blends with the cotton wool, takes on its texture and colour. Someone is pushing me. With great effort I tear open my eyes. Mary is bending over me, a folded wing under each arm. Or are they broken wings?

"You're alright now. It was only a bad dream!" Her grey hair is tousled. She's wearing a grey nightshirt with long sleeves and looks like an old angel. "An old fallen angel", I mumble.

She prods my arm. "Wake up! You're still dreaming!"

Why did I say "fallen"? "Are you afraid of them?" I ask.

"You're still not awake!" She shakes me gently.

"Mary, there's something I must ask you. Did they ever ... I mean, were you ever ..." The question is too monstrous. I can't put it into words.

Mary pats my hand. "Wait 'til morning when we'll both be properly awake."

The next morning, embarrassed, I avoid her, leave very early and spend the day at the hospice. There's no change. Still anxious to continue my search, I start off directly after tea. Daylight is beginning to fade and I mustn't linger. Every moment might be precious. This time I will go to the nearby strand. We often went there, my sister and I.

When I reach it, I discover that a strip of land has been reclaimed to accommodate a new long stretch of lawn. Benches have been installed here and there, so that now one can sit while looking out over the sea at the two distant peninsulas where, on the left, Howth Head rises, and on the right, Bray Head. Tonight, as so often in the past, mist envelops both. They used to form the backdrop to our daydreams. My sister's were concrete, logical. She would become a great scholar, correct the world, make important contributions. There was so much to be put right. She'd climb the Head to the left. At the top she would meet a man who was charming, cultured and intelligent. They'd have wonderful exchanges.

I couldn't tell her my dreams, couldn't decode them for her. They sprang from a mysterious place inside me. She'd laugh at me if I tried to explain. So, to please her, I said I dreamed of climbing the Head on the right and in the mist at the top I'd find Jean, a boy left behind in France, beyond the seas we'd had to cross. And Jean would carry me back with him because I loved France, and my love had made it mine.

My sister tried not to laugh at this childish dream. Why should Jean carry me? And loving a place or a person gave one no claim to them. She was right of course. Still, wasn't it simply a matter of semantics? Loving something or someone does make them become a part of you forever, even when that love is rejected. That was what I'd meant by "making it mine". But I phrased it badly, couldn't match her clarity.

The old gap in the seawall is still there, as are the broken steps leading down to the water. Tonight the tide is out. The water has only just receded. The soggy sand glistens in the twilight and my shoes sink in at every step. I take them off.

My bare feet curl over and into the pattern left behind by waves and crush little mounds of curly worm castings. With the smell of iodine in my nostrils, I make my way toward the old baths, a cement enclosure already abandoned when we knew it as children. At high tide, when big waves splashed over the wall on to the street and caught passers-by unawares, only the baths' rim showed above the water. We came in our bathing suits and ran in. How warm the sea felt when it rained! My sister was a strong swimmer and struck out at once with smooth, regular strokes. I'd never learned to swim and waded clumsily in her wake, feeling stupid and inept, but also deeply happy at being in the same water with her.

The old baths were so far away from everything else that, near it, privacy felt complete. We waited to speak until we reached them. Only then, in the shelter of their wall, did we share secrets. This was where my sister confided to me things which she later refused to dwell on and severely forbade me to mention.

Surely, if my sister is also looking for me, she'll expect to find me there, in that place of old shared intimacies. This was where we spoke about that other man, the one who took us in, who pretended to be concerned only with our welfare. I well remembered his hurting us, but I was too young to understand. I remembered feeling very sick afterwards, for months. Still, I didn't understand. Not fully, even when my sister told me all, perched on the wall of the old baths, its sharp rim cutting into our thighs and our memories.

In daylight, the walls show stains and dark watermarks. Now, in moonlight, they stand out bright. A shadow moves along them. I run toward it but find nothing. I go round the full square of the baths. Still nothing.

A cloud is moving across the moon and it is quite dark underfoot. I cut my foot on a sharp shell and limp back toward the sodium street-lamps. Their pink is changing to an eerie yellow.

My sister never came to this strand with me. She wouldn't allow herself to be seen in a bathing suit from the street. She knew better than to expose herself. She swam only in secluded coves, further along the coast. Then where did we share those intimacies? Or did we ever?

It is late when I return to the house. I am free to come and go as I please. No restrictions are imposed. Why does it remind me of that other house of long ago?

The following morning, when Mary hears that I am setting out for the Dublin mountains, she makes sure I take a packed lunch. "There's no place for miles around where you could get a bite", she says.

"Then it hasn't changed!"

I'm relieved. If it is still as we knew it, retracing our steps of long ago will be easier.

It's raining now with quiet insistence, silver drops clinging to the tips of leaves. I follow the road along the banks of the Dodder, soft with moss, then go up, up into the mountains along walled country roads. There are sudden flashes of yellow gorse around me. In this country, surprises sprout from the earth all year.

The wind is just as strong as I remember, but the slopes seem steeper. Clouds reflect the purple velvet of the mountains. It's all achingly familiar. I find the old ruins of what might once have been a small house of worship and touch the wet stones of former walls. No doubt they were blessed in the name of a deity by the people who assem-bled them and prayed in their confines. So many holy places are built on mountain tops. So many spiritual visions are glimpsed there. All through the ages in every culture, man has sought out heights to feel closer to a God. In both hemispheres, one pointing up, the other down!

Sudden laughter rings out. I scramble to my feet and look around. There's no one in sight. Then I realize it is Professor C's laughter, the laughter I would have heard, had he been there to share my thought about the two hemispheres. He used to love such paradoxes. "If heaven lies in every direction, where can hell be, right?" he'd have elaborated with a chuckle.

Except for a very occasional hiker, we hardly ever met a soul. We'd lean our bicycles against some gate, pick blackberries and, higher up, searched out blueberries under their red-tinted leaves. Water gurgles its way downward as it did then. At the top where it was windy, we looked down at the green valley threaded with silver streams. We didn't speak. There was no need. Becoming part of this landscape was an end in itself.

The silence between my sister and me was special. We had long since given up our secret language. We needed no words, were able to communicate across hundreds of miles without them. A whole country and two seas lay between us on the night she dreamt that I fell downstairs shortly before I actually did. Best of all was when we had the same dream at the same time.

Then why do I feel she doesn't want to see me? Only because she said so, and words are so often not what they seem. The very last time we spoke she said she wondered what is worth preserving. And suddenly I know.

Professor C. claimed that we each carry one book within us, whether we write it or not. Now I think about my sister's book. It is bound to consist in part of our shared experiences, but our perceptions of them must differ greatly. Does such a book undergo constant changes while it's within us? Does it reach maturity and then decline at the same rate we do? Only when it's free of the body, frozen into the written form, can it remain unchanged. This thought, too, would have provoked Prof. C's laughter. I recall how fond he was of saying, "It's enough to read just one book in a lifetime, provided it's the right book!" He did not say that it had to be someone else's! The old rogue! The laughter that rings out this time is my own. And suddenly I hear my sister laugh too. Enormous relief floods through me as I remember her laughter. It will guide me.

I go back to the hospice and find her. At last. Her eyes are still firmly shut. She cannot speak. But she can hear. I simply know that she can. I can speak to her. At last. The frown that so often furrowed her brow is gone. Her features are unwrinkled and relaxed. I want to kiss her. But she never liked her face to be touched. Instead, I take her hand in mine. It feels firm, strong, as does her arm. I stroke it but remain silent. My voice would betray me. I am the past and she wants no part of it. A strong urge to say "I love you!" fights its way up my throat. But we never said that to one another. We were not brought up to say it. It was something that went without saying.

The passing is easy. Too easy. It simply has not happened. I find her and lose her in one and the same moment.

Mary buys me white lilies. She has never met my sister, only knows of her existence through me. She says she is very sorry for my loss.

Quickly I say, "My sister and I were often separated." I don't want to look at the flowers. I don't want sympathy. I don't want to hear the word "loss".

But Mary goes on, "Loss is also liberating."

"Liberating" shocks me even more than "loss".

"My sister has ..." I begin. But I cannot say it. I cannot mouth the words.

"My sister is still ... of the living", I say in my sister's voice.

GERMANY:

A RETURN

Not long after the Berlin Wall had come down, I was invited to give a series of readings in Germany. I had not been back there since we fled to France in the early 1930s and the prospect of a return after so many years was bewildering. I was curious to see the country, to experience it anew and meet German people. At the same time, I felt a strong reluctance to do any of those things.

I reasoned with myself. Over half a century had elapsed. It was wrong to dwell on ancient history. One had to move on. The world had changed – but do people? I would be staying with kind Canadian friends and so, in the end, I did go.

Unexpectedly, it proved to be a very emotional encounter. On one hand it felt completely natural to be there, but on the other I was a stranger. I understood every word that was spoken and knew enough German to reply and interact, but my tongue would not obey. It was completely irrational but I felt as if I choked on the words. My itinerary consisted of visits to a number of university towns where I was to meet staff members, give readings and speak to the students. Knowing that everyone was more or less fluent in English, I told the students during the first few days that they were welcome to put questions to me in German but that I would reply in English. This helped me over the initial hurdle.

My tour began in Jena where the first of my hosts, while walking me to his class at the University, asked me to tell the students that I was Jewish and then speak specifically of my early history. I saw no reason to dwell on my own past and protested, saying that surely my name spoke for itself. He apologized but insisted, explaining that he wanted the students to be made aware of what Germany's recent past had included. Most of them had never met a Jew, perhaps none had, nor had they at school learned about the genocide. This stain, he said, was entirely omitted from their history books. Of course, I could then no longer refuse.

It was difficult to gauge what impact my revelations had on the class as a whole. My own extreme discomfort in that situation no doubt affected some of them too. At least two or three showed genuine concern, in particular one student in Erlangen/Nuremberg, who asked to speak to me privately later. I agreed and he offered to walk me round Nuremberg. He was a tour guide in his spare time, he explained.

We met the next afternoon and walked extensively and talked. He had planned the walk carefully and pointed out sites of historical or other interest as we passed them. He was a history student and well-informed. This was, after all, the very city where in 1935, Hitler had called parliament into a special session at the annual Nazi rally, to pass two laws that would provide the legal framework for the systematic persecution of Jews. But my student friend said he had been unable to relate to these happenings. He was born after it was all over, and those events felt unreal, disembodied – or rather, had felt unreal until now. Until he met me. This worried me greatly.

We reached a very large square where, he explained, there had been many massacres of Jews. I asked, "Under Hitler?" No, he said, in the year 1298, and again in 1349 when horrible pogroms were carried out expressly to clear the area of any Jews who lived there, thus making room for a market place. He was most contrite and hoped he had not upset me too much with these revelations. He said that meeting me, getting to know me and liking me, had put a face on what had been an abstraction to him before. My presence had brought the victims to life.

Before we parted, he asked could he write to me. Of course I said yes and, on arriving home, found a twelve-page letter from him waiting for me. In it he mentioned, among other things, a particular poem of mine that I had read to his class, which he felt was addressed to him. Of course, it was not, having been published before we met. The following is part of my response to him.

September, 1993. Letter to M.

Thank you for your gently probing letter.

I would like to put your mind at rest about my visit to Nuremberg. In spite of its history, it was neither more nor less painful for me than visiting any other part of Germany. It is alas, difficult for me to dissociate the recent past from any part of the country and to feel at ease ... This unease is fed by daily events reported in the media and the consequent spectre they raise: how quickly and easily could it all happen again? ...

If there is any hope, and we must pray there is, it rests with you and people like you.

During my stay in Germany I met with kindness and concern on the part of many people. The difficulty on both sides lies in our inability to put events into perspective in a global and historical sense. The imme-diacy of personal contact overshadows all else.

Your meeting one person like me is probably not much help. Perhaps, to a certain extent, it makes the issue less abstract for you. But your perception of me and whatever you feel about me, will inevitably be your guide. You may like my face and find me "sympathisch" (likable; engaging). But what if you did not? Or if, on further acquaintance, you came to dislike me? How would you then feel about those victims? Would you suddenly see them differently? As being undeserving? ... This is by no means an accusation. I am merely pointing out the unreliable way in which the human psyche works – yours, mine, everybody's. The tendency is always to generalize.

I fully agree that there is no value in collective guilt feelings. One's stand must rest on one's own evaluation and yes, by all means, a sense of individual responsibility for the future – although we are, alas, all too helpless in the face of political intrigue, mass manipulation and last but not least, the financial interests which govern the world.

Your wish to teach history in its entirety is highly commendable. The best one can hope to do is to present it in as objective a form as possible, which I know you will do. With luck, you will have students who, like you, will condemn horrors perpetrated at home as well as abroad. But others, for a variety of reasons, will let prejudice guide them. Still, it is teachers like you who will, in the end, make it possible for sanity to prevail.

I'm glad you found me to be free of hate. It's true that, to the best of my knowledge, I don't harbour any. Nor do I, in all honesty, feel bitterness about the past. But I am horrified and deeply saddened by man's tragic inhumanity to man, past and present. People of many different races, creeds and colour are guilty of similar crimes – only the scale and manner in which they are committed varies.

In the poem you took so personally, with "Part and counterpart", I did mean, as you rightly guessed, that "we" are two related parts, not identical, but possibly interchangeable.

And yes, I must confess to feeling doubt about our ability to change ourselves … This makes me cynical, not bitter. Cynicism leaves room for hope. Bitterness does not.

I hope that these clarifications will show the poem to be more of a universal condemnation than was your impression.

Thank you for your thoughtful questions. Do write me whenever the spirit moves you.

Warmest good wishes,
Inge

MARK

We were blessed with two wonderful children one of whom was taken from us, an event that will forever feel raw, that I can never accept. A child is part of one, of one's heart and mind and soul. One does not, cannot lose it.

I carry my son in me as if he were yet to be born. I cannot outlive him.

Accident

Bursting into the ICU, straight
from the airport, we find you prostrate,
staples and stitches close your skull,
large screws your pelvis.
Gashes everywhere. Fatal,
they say. Touch and go, they say.
A respirator breathes for you, rhythmic,
unnatural, your dear, dear familiar
features waxen. Can this
really be you? More handsome
than even I remember. Larger
than I remember, your legs longer
than the bed. Your eyes firmly shut.
Mine linger over the curve of your brows,
your long lashes. Then I see the blood
in your ears. Oh, my love,
don't leave us!

We're led to a private room. Inside,
the trauma surgeon says they can keep you
alive – as long as we want them to.
Then asks, do we want them to?
How can such a question be asked?
Or mouthed?
How can it be answered?
The enormity of it allows for no words.
No language will do. It's a knife
at one's choking throat and the surgeon
sits still and waits.
His eyes don't connect with ours.
How could they?

Beside you again, I musn't sob.
In case you hear. The present,
the past, a kaleidoscope
where a myriad memories topple over
one another, are shaken into different
patterns, briefly flash before me,
are gone.

What was the pain of bringing you
into this world to the pain
of taking you out of it?

Only twelve that summer day, you ran
shaken, into your room
and shut the door. I followed,
knocked. You'd thrown yourself
on the bed, face ashen on the pillow.
"Please", I begged, "please share it
to make it lighter." I stroked your hand
as I'm doing now. Long minutes
later, shards of words cut
their way out between dry sobs.
A squirrel. Run over. Not quite.
Still moving. Barely. So you'd ridden
your bike. Over it. Stopped its
suffering. You – the gentlest of
creatures – had done this violence,
were shaken to the core. I held you tight.
So brave, I said.

But, oh my love, how could we
say this to the surgeon,
the one who said you stand
next to no chance
of a meaningful recovery?

When Luca Signorelli's son was brought
to him from a tavern brawl, not yet quite
cold, he asked that the body be laid
out before him on his bed, tore off

the boy's blood-drenched clothes, took
up his pencil and all night long drew
his son's features, the beauty
of his head, the glory of his limbs,
to have and to hold,
to lend to saints and angels
he would later paint in frescoes
on cathedral walls, in the TESTAMENT
OF MOSES at the Sistine Chapel,
in THE LAST JUDGMENT,
in THE END OF THE WORLD.

How could he? I used to wonder.
What kind of father could be
so utterly unfeeling?
So cold and calculating?

But am I not equally guilty? Sitting
by your bedside, pinning down
these living memories
as would a collector of butterflies,
their wings still fluttering?

As if we were stepping through
Alice's LOOKING GLASS, you held
my hand, showed me San Diego;
from overpasses, the unstoppable
red lava flow in one direction,
black in the other, of traffic;
OLD TOWN, California's cradle. Proud
of the new job, of how fine a place

this is, you reassured me," ... so safe:
it's beyond the St Andreas faultline,
the most threatened earthquake zone!";
pointing at happy joggers, at "safe"
cycle paths, everything so bright!
But in a single moment's inattention
the van rammed into you, and pitched
you into darkness.

Days turn into weeks, weeks into months.
Tinder-dry eucalyptus wait, condemned
at the sun's stake, wounded hillsides
crumble under unsuspecting houses,
exhaust fumes blot out the sky
and greying, yellowing palms are helpless
dirty mops weeping dust tears
but none, NONE of this matters now
while your heart rate shoots up,
your oxygen intake falters,
your left hand, though it can't move,
clenches vice-like until my fingers
turn blue and you, my darling, teeter
on the razor-edge between this world
and some other.

Beeping, ticking monitors attached
to you like marine predators
register pressures, vital signs.
Now and then an alarm goes off.
Your eyes open differently –
oh joy! It must mean ...?

But they're not aligned, one pupil
is larger than the other and they don't
close when a hand is passed over them.
It doesn't count.

Now ... NOW you're stretching your arms
downward along your body. Surely ...
but no, it's called posturing, a purely
involuntary movement. It doesn't count.

Our bus to the hospital passes through
downtown San Diego. Around the Courthouse,
bail bond adverts shriek at us, "WE'LL MEET
YOU AT ANY TIME, IN ANY JAIL!"
Would that they could spring you
from your isolation cell!

Standing beside you I try and try
to pry open your clenched hand, finally
succeed only to have you reclench it
over my thumb just as incredibly hard.
Where does that amazing strength come
from – when the rest of you is totally
limp? Again I struggle. "Please relax",
I say quiely, over and over as I pull
at your fingers with my other hand
and suddenly the whole building shakes.
A quake – only 5.4 on the Richter scale -
still, unsettling. The staff has quickly
assembled in the hall. Is more to come?

Our hands still locked, I wonder: if you
knew, would your great sense of humour save
the moment? Would you say, "You see,
it's perfectly safe!"

So many intrusive hands, some
skilful, some rough, touch every part
of you, and you always so painfully
shy, so fiercely private, lie here
barely covered during these days
of endless hours, months of endless
weeks, while oxygen is pumped
into the base of your throat
and liquid food into your stomach.
We stand beside you or perch
on the edge of seats, every nerve
taut, every muscle tense, ready
to spring forward at an instant,
waiting, powerless, cannot formulate
hope, dare not pray. Which deity
would hear us? We have lost all sense
of time and place, try to make
conversation, to reorient ourselves,
quote statistics: thirty thousand
people die every day, sixty thousand
are born. Earthquakes occur here,
there, everywhere. Terrorist acts.
Wars. But nothing reconnects us
with the world outside.

Are the old beacons of your mind
like distant used-up stars
which no longer exist
although the memory of their light
still travels toward us?

Are your thought patterns part
of our knowable universe
or do they inhabit a different
realm? If your injured brain
is building new neuronal paths
in place of those destroyed, making
new connections, how will you
interpret what reaches you
through the all-enveloping fog?
How will you see this world
that failed you?

Outside on the high wire,
a mockingbird sings out loud and clear
in the voices of other birds.
And you, my darling, if you come back
to us, who will you be?

I am no longer sure of anything
as you plane in regions beyond
my understanding. How insignificant
the learning of a lifetime before
the immensity of the distance
now separating us! And yet I've never
felt more at one with you. The pulsing
tremor in your hand governs the rhythm
of my breath. Away from you, at night

in bed, it's your rapid eye movement
I feel behind my eyelids,

it's the stiffness in your neck
that tilts my head awkwardly
on my pillow, and my fingers traveling
over my blanket are yours, exploring
your hospital gown in clumsy attempts
to find the tubes invading your body.
We stroke and massage your neck, lift
your limbs, rotate your feet, toes,
fingers, try to teach you to use them
not only in involuntary gestures
but wilfully, to make them your own.

Morning dawns after morning but brings
no change. I can't go on. I go on.
Like the mother pelican who, unable
to bring food to her young, rips open
her belly to let them feed on her
innards, I want to rip off my head
and offer you the contents.

The respirator breathes for you but also
harms you. It must be removed,
replaced by a traecheotomy
– that will rob you of your voice,
not only your fine basso profundo
but any sound, any speech.

You are silent in any case, more silent
even than ... I almost said than in life.
But you ARE alive! Your heart IS beating.
And mine keeps time with yours.
Oh, my darling, please wake up!

In this smaller hospital where you
have been moved, other patients lie
in comas at various categorized levels.
The man injured in a fire, reached
stage three when he began to scream
and shout, at first intermittently,
now day and night. Screaming should be
your next level. Your eyes, wild
when open, plead dumbly, desperately.
But you show no signs of readiness
when they try to cap the opening
at the base of your throat. You never
screamed before, at any age –
so would you, could you do so now?
Do you KNOW how to vent fear, anger,
frustration? If not, is it my doing?
Did I deprive you of that safety valve?
Please, my darling, forgive me
if I did. I never meant to muzzle you!
"They mess you up, your Mom and Dad!"*
But not intentionally. NEVER!

What wouldn't I give to hear you rant
and rave, shout and scream at the top
of your lungs, to hear you mouthe

obscenities! Yes! And the worst
of curses, to use your lungs
to their great and full capacity,
in your basso profundo voice.

My best friend lost a sister – we were
thirteen. "We mustn't laugh
in her presence, it would hurt her!"
I said to those who giggled at school.
But she returned unchanged, smiling,
cheerful, eager as ever to get sweets
at the tuck-shop. Why wasn't she grief
– stricken, tongue-tied, why not sad?
How could she think of sweets?
Hadn't she loved her sister?

But now we too somehow continue
to eat, even to sleep. How can we?
You lie here helpless, my darling,
a ragdoll, at the mercy of all
these tubes, fevers come and go,
pneumonias, thromboses ... how can we
bear to leave you for a single moment?
Night hours are quicksand where you
and I drown, the umbilical cord
unsevered. Dawn brings no relief.
That's when executioners ply their trade.

What an explosive blow your poor head
suffered! Your brow is a delicate cage.
During brief respite from pain, do tiny
birds sing in the deep valleys
of your mind, the closed-off regions
beyond our reach, beyond yours? Or is it
all chaos ... as was the early universe
after the big bang? In moments of great
agitation, when your pulse races, when
you look not just frightened
but terrified, I can feel your world
convulsing, there's no delving
into the past or reaching toward a future.
You're doing battle with furious versions
of the here and now.

You never spoke about yourself to us.
Never. Why? A wound? A word?
Because of us – your parents?
A door jumps out from shadows,
then jumps away. From under the bed
ominous shapes tear free, intermingle,
crawl out of sight.

I see you little, skipping along
by my side so trustingly
and I can no more unsee those images
than undream this hospital room.
Will you come back to us, my love?

Your mouth is sealed, your voice
silenced but sometimes you appear
to listen, sometimes your eyes
seem to gaze into mine.

Quickly, I offer you handfuls
of cherished memories - oh,
how cherished! Or pour you
little bowls of song from those
we used to sing. I look
into your gentle, kind eyes,
my voice cracks
but, just for you,
I manage to sculpt
a smile from the granite
in my breast.

* *A line from a poem by Philip Larkin*